Talking Teenagers

by the same author

Parent to Parent
Information and Inspiration for Parents Dealing with Autism
and Asperger's Syndrome
Ann Boushéy
ISBN-13: 978 1 84310 774 3   ISBN-10: 1 84310 774 0

of related interest

Parenting Across the Autism Spectrum
Unexpected Lessons We Have Learned
Maureen F. Morrell and Ann Palmer
ISBN-13: 978 1 84310 807 8   ISBN-10: 1 84310 807 0

That's Life with Autism
Tales and Tips for Families with Autism
Edited by Donna Satterlee Ross and Kelly Ann Jolly
ISBN-13: 978 1 84310 829 0   ISBN-10: 1 84310 829 1

Asperger Syndrome in Adolescence
Living with the Ups, the Downs, and Things in Between
Edited by Liane Holliday Willey
Foreword by Luke Jackson
ISBN-13: 978 1 84310 742 2   ISBN-10: 1 84310 742 2

Asperger's Syndrome
A Guide for Parents and Professionals
Tony Attwood
Foreword by Lorna Wing
ISBN-13: 978 1 85302 577 8   ISBN-10: 1 85302 577 1

The Complete Guide to Asperger's Syndrome
Tony Attwood
ISBN-13: 978 1 84310 495 7   ISBN-10: 1 84310 495 4

Freaks, Geeks and Asperger Syndrome
A User Guide to Adolescence
Luke Jackson
Foreword by Tony Attwood
ISBN-13: 978 1 84310 098 0   ISBN-10: 1 84310 098 3

Survival Strategies for People on the Autism Spectrum
Marc Fleisher
ISBN-13: 978 1 84310 261 8   ISBN-10: 1 84310 261 7

Being Bullied
Strategies and Solutions for People with Asperger's Syndrome
Nick Dubin
ISBN-13: 978 1 84310 843 6   ISBN-10: 1 84310 843 7   DVD

Asperger Syndrome and Employment
A Personal Guide to Succeeding at Work
Nick Dubin
With Gail Hawkins
ISBN-13: 978 1 84310 849 8   ISBN-10: 1 84310 849 6   DVD

Talking Teenagers
Information and Inspiration for Parents of Teenagers with Autism or Asperger's Syndrome

Ann Boushéy

Jessica Kingsley Publishers
London and Philadelphia

First published in 2007
by Jessica Kingsley Publishers
116 Pentonville Road
London N1 9JB, UK
and
400 Market Street, Suite 400
Philadelphia, PA 19106, USA

www.jkp.com

Library of Congress Cataloging in Publication Data
Boushéy, Ann, 1957-
   Talking teenagers : information and inspiration for parents of teenagers with autism or Asperger's syndrome / Ann Boushéy.
      p. cm.
   Includes bibliographical references and index.
   ISBN-13: 978-1-84310-844-3 (pbk. : alk. paper)
   ISBN-10: 1-84310-844-5 (pbk. : alk. paper) 1. Autism in adolescence. 2. Asperger's syndrome in adolescence. 3. Parents of autistic children. I. Title.
   RJ506.A9B683 2007
   618.92'858832--dc22

                                                                    2006036725

British Library Cataloguing in Publication Data
A CIP catalogue record for this book is available from the British Library

ISBN-13: 978 1 84310 844 3
ISBN-10: 1 84310 844 5

Printed and bound in the United States by
Thomson-Shore, Inc.

This book is dedicated to Jon, my own teen, who inspires me, challenges me, and continues to amaze me, but also dedicated to a young teen who came to my first book signing. She had just been diagnosed Asperger's at age thirteen, was full of questions about my son and amazed that she and he were so much alike. When her mom told her they had to leave and make room for others in line, she started to cry and tried to hug me and thank me. This book is dedicated to her for touching my heart, and for many, many autistic and Asperger's teenagers out there whose hearts I hope to touch by showing them that they too are not the only ones.

Acknowledgements

My son Jon and his friend Alex (not on the spectrum) lent their photo for the front cover, and the reading and editing team of J. & J. Prince worked long and hard over drafts of this manuscript. Thank you to Jessica Kingsley for allowing me to share my story in hopes of helping others worldwide.

Disclaimer

This work is my story, my words, and my opinion. It should in no way be taken as an expert's opinion. I am only an expert in my own son's case.

Contents

A little knowledge that acts is worth infinitely more than much knowledge that is idle.

(Kahlil Gibran 1883–1931)

Introduction

All the interests of my reason, speculative as well as practical,
combine in the three following questions: 1. What can I
know? 2. What ought I to do? 3. What may I hope?
(Immanuel Kant 1793, German philosopher)

What does an eighteenth-century German philosopher have to do with a
parent of a teenager with autism or Asperger's Syndrome? Kant is one of
my favorite philosophers. He changed the philosophy of his day with his
revolutionary ideas on thought, knowledge and God, without traveling
any further than 50 miles from his home. In our day of wanting to go,
and see, to learn and do, I find this fact amazing; and I wonder—can I
emulate this philosopher?

It seems I've internalized Kant's three questions without being
conscious of the fact: *What can I know? What ought I to do? What may I
hope?* All of these have been circling in my mind for the past decade.

Ten years ago, when my son Jon was diagnosed as high-functioning
autistic (or, as his first IEP [Individual Education Plan] stated
"autistic-like"), these questions, along with about a million others began
to dominate my thinking. Soon I realized that, for me, *knowledge* brought
peace. Thus, I set out as most parents will do, in a search of knowledge,
trying to answer the swirling questions.

Some questions were examined in my first book, *Parent to Parent:
Information and Inspiration for Parents Dealing with Autism or Asperger's
Syndrome* (2004). There I pulled together information I had found during
my search and shared it, along with inspiration, in the hopes of helping
another parent or educator going through what I had gone through. But
after that book was finished, did my questions go away?

Let me answer this with another question: Is my son still autistic? I
may have found many answers along the way, but the questions have not
stopped.

Our family is a pretty typical family. We live in the mid-west, and both my husband and I work full time. Jon, although doing well, is still autistic, but now he is a *teenager*. So in addition to his autism behaviors changing, his life has changed, along with his needs and wants because of his age.

I've come to realize that Jon is a teenager first, someone with autism second. So my years of questions and issues have suddenly regrouped themselves. I have to be talking and focusing on teen issues, but autism affects everything. I found myself in quicksand and sinking fast. So, I did what I do best. I researched, read, and tried to keep up with him.

What follows are some of the questions, and answers, I've had as my son has grown into a teen. However, as in real life, most questions generally lead to another. Those other questions are here also.

Whether it's practical advice, interviewing the experts, or more personal issues, this book contains a little of what I've found in dealing with my teenage son, and autism. My first book was the early years, this could be considered the latter. Who knows what will follow when we get to young adulthood?

As in my first book, after each chapter I have a "Chicken nugget for the soul." These nuggets came about because during the first four to six years of my son's life, all he would eat was chicken nuggets—any shape, any kind, just the nuggets. It was enough to drive any parent crazy. So the nuggets are here to encourage parents to stay sane. They contain small bits of information, points of inspiration, thoughts to let you know you are not alone as you try to find your answers.

If you are a parent, or an educator, I encourage you to take this journey with me, through these questions and answers. My purpose here is not to resolve issues, but to look at them, try to answer them, and empower others to do the same. And perhaps as Kant did, influence others without traveling more than 50 miles from home.

While others may be "talking shop" we are "talking teenagers," because the questions haven't gone away, they've only changed.

Chapter One

A parent's heartache—ever present

Endure my heart: you once endured something even more dreadful.

(Homer)

Will my heart ever stop breaking?

I know of a family who is dealing with "shaken baby syndrome." I've read that the neurological symptoms of this syndrome are similar to autism spectrum disorder, so I spoke to the adoptive mom and was able to share a little bit about my son Jon and autism. We talked about school districts, and I detailed how she could get help for her preschool-aged child, *before* he gets to kindergarten.

As a result of our brief conversation, he is now getting physical and occupational therapy, not to mention that the adoptive grandparents are taking an informed and active role in his life. So it was no surprise to me when the grandmother stopped by to talk. But the first words out of her mouth took me aback. "Will my heart ever stop breaking?" she asked, her eyes filling with tears.

She explained that since her daughter ran a home daycare, she, grandma, was the one taking her grandson to a music therapy group. She said it was very difficult first to get him to go into the room and participate, and then to sit in a circle with the other kids for the entire session. I explained about Jon's sensitive hearing, and that perhaps her grandson was hearing too much during the session. We talked about moving him away from the circle a little, to keep stimulation down, so he could possibly sit through the entire class.

The next time we spoke, she said she tried this, but he wouldn't sit any distance away from the group. In fact, he wanted to sit very close to the teacher's side, stuck to her like glue. He still became very agitated and ended up having to leave the music sessions with grandma.

"And you know," she said, "sitting and watching the group, with all of the other parents watching him…it just breaks your heart…" This time she wasn't able to finish her thought, but she didn't need to.

I understood what she was trying to say. She, grandma, loved her new grandson very much, and it gave her such heartache to see other parents watching him as he struggled in this music group, but what could she do? Would her heart ever stop breaking?—No, I thought.

Jon is in his teens, and does it still bother me, at times break my heart, to see him struggle in a situation as others watch him?—Yes.

At the end of Jon's seventh grade, we received a letter inviting us to the seventh grade awards assembly. Only those students who would be getting an award for their grades were invited to attend, and we were excited for Jon. We knew his grade point average was high, but we had never attended an awards assembly before. Alas, I wish I had called and asked someone to explain this assembly to me in detail.

We arrived at the front entrance to see a large crowd of students, parents, and teachers milling around. I stuck my head in the gym and noticed the students were taking seats in chairs on the gym floor, while the parents climbed up into the stands. This would immediately be a challenge since Jon would have to sit through the assembly on the floor with the students, and not next to us. I stopped one of the teachers, had this confirmed, and carefully explained the situation to Jon.

"No. I'll sit with you," was his first response.

I thought this over for a minute and decided no, he could sit with the rest of the students. I walked out onto the floor with him and told him to look and see if he knew any of the other students in the chairs.

"No one," he said.

This didn't surprise me. It's difficult for Jon to look people in the face, so he rarely connects people and faces. I wandered around a bit and found three boys and an empty chair. They recognized me from my previous years of substitute teaching and I asked them if they minded Jon sitting next to them. Nods and shrugs, and soon he was seated at the end of a row next to, according to him, "total strangers." My husband and I were relegated to the stands and the assembly began.

Jon was fine in the opening moments of the assembly; he sat straight in his chair and even seemed to be paying attention. When the principal explained that he would read the names of the seventh grade honor role students and they should all stand, I began to get worried. Would Jon hear his name? Would he stand? I noticed after this announcement Jon was asking the boy next to him a question, which the boy answered. Jon's name, beginning with a "B" was one of the first. He stood up. I was so proud of him. But then instead of standing along with the other students, he quickly sat back down. Thus, when the parents were told to applaud the seventh grade honor roll students, he was sitting, slumped in his chair with his hands over his ears.

The assembly went downhill from there. It was long, consisting of individual student awards, and Jon sunk lower and lower in his seat. At one point he turned completely around in his chair and faced the opposite direction. I watched my son, knowing I couldn't do anything to correct his behavior, and wondering if other parents were noticing him too. By the end of the assembly he was doubled over in his seat and had his arms over his head.

My heart was breaking for him... I could tell he was miserable and yet at the same time, I wondered how other parents saw him. Spoiled? Rude? Perhaps odd that he couldn't sit like a seventh grader through an entire assembly?

When it was over, my husband and I became separated by the crush of parents, and from my view on the steps, I could see my husband wandering around on the gym floor. He walked right past Jon, not seeing him doubled up in his seat, while all of the other students were up, out of their chairs, hurrying around.

When I arrived on the scene, my husband had turned around, noticed Jon still sitting in his chair, and we arrived at Jon's side together. Jon looked up and his face was red. He was holding back tears.

"What's wrong?" I asked.

"I thought I was going to get an award?" he whispered.

I hadn't realized that he wasn't aware that when his name was called with all of the other honor role students, and the parents applauded, this was his recognition. Jon hadn't followed what the principal had said, he just knew that he didn't get to go up to the front and get a handshake and a piece of paper handed to him like the individual awards that were given.

My heart broke again. I began to explain the assembly to him, and was momentarily interrupted by Jon's math teacher, who approached to tell me what a good job Jon had done in his class this year. My husband and I thanked him and Jon tried to nod.

On the way out to the car, we explained it all again. At the local McDonald's where we stopped for ice cream, we tried to explain it a different way. By the time we were home he was better and he seemed to have forgotten his upset.

The next day when I picked him up at school he came out to the car with a huge grin on his face, waving a piece of paper.

"Mom! I got my award. I told you I would get one!"

Sure enough. He had a printed certificate, stating that he had made seventh grade honor role. Evidently there had been too many to hand out individually the night before, so they had sent them home the next day.

"I told you!" he repeated.

I smiled. This time my heart ached in a good way. I was so happy that *he* was happy!

So, does it go away? This heartache?—No!

It will be there throughout your child's life, because you love him and he is your heart. You wish others would not look at him or her differently, this child of your heart. But the fact is, your child *is* different. If you took the time to explain to every person watching your child what those differences were, you would run out of time and probably miss some good moments along the way.

Perhaps we need to learn not to worry about what other people are thinking, but, more importantly, change our thinking? Next time I go to an event where others are watching my son, I will beam with pride, and remind myself how far he has come in his young life. After all, it wasn't too long ago he wouldn't even enter a crowded gym, much less sit through an assembly by himself. If he is displaying inappropriate behavior, I will trust that those watching him may have an inkling, that Jon is a student with differences. I will not assume that they are thinking bad things about my son's behavior. Maybe they aren't even noticing him?

Virginia Woolf wrote at the end of her life, "The beauty of the world has two edges...one of laughter, one of anguish, cutting the heart asunder." Our hearts ache in bad times and in good. It's the way we as parents are made. My heart is cut asunder.

If I learned to embrace this heartache, would it make my life easier?

HFA or AS? What's the diff?

As my son has grown older and matured, I have wondered, *is* there a difference between high-functioning autism (HFA) and Asperger's Syndrome (AS)?

I looked to the experts for the answer to this and found an article posted at www.autism.info/munro.html. Nell Munro, an Autism Helpline worker, compiled a list in 1999 comparing the two. Munro explains that Leo Kanner began to define infantile autism in the 1940s, at about the same time Austrian Hans Asperger began studying similar conditions in his own patients. But at first he referred to these patients as having a personality disorder. While Kanner was widely read and published in English both in the US and UK, Asperger was mostly ignored in the English-speaking world. Much later, Asperger argued that he and Kanner had discovered two entirely different syndromes. However, when studies by Gould and Wing came out in the late 1970s describing autism as a condition that existed along a spectrum of disorders, this argument was partially put to rest. Most experts then concluded that both Kanner and Asperger had been studying the same disorders in children, only calling them something different.

One can still find those who feel there are differences in several areas of the two, for example: level of cognitive functioning, motor skills, language development and age of onset. There are also some who say that IQ and prognosis are what sets the two apart.

After reading and researching, my opinion as a parent is that this issue is one of those ongoing arguments in the scientific world that I can't allow to sidetrack me.

My son was diagnosed, high-functioning autistic, or autistic-like. But when I read, for example, the excellent book by Tony Attwood titled *Asperger's Syndrome: A Guide for Parents and Professionals* (1998), my son fits right in. Yet, when reading Dr. Temple Grandin's *Thinking in Pictures* (1996), where she states that she feels she is autistic not Asperger's, he fits into her world too. As always, we have to decide unresolved issues individually, to our own satisfaction, and see how these issues affect our children.

What I know for sure is that changing Jon's diagnosis at this stage of the game, already into high school, will not change the services he is getting through the school system. And it's highly possible that since HFA is a more common diagnosis and more educators are gaining understanding of autism, changing his diagnosis to Asperger's Syndrome now could be detrimental.

Asperger's Syndrome is now becoming better understood, but in the US some states do not list it as a disability. Just as every youth is an individual on the spectrum, every school, and situation is different. Thus, I feel a parent must be very careful in switching a diagnosis mid-stream.

As a result I write this book for parents who are working with either diagnosis. The experts are still trying to resolve the issue. In the meantime, I'm determined not to get weighed down by it, and to continue to try to only do what is best for Jon. But now I wonder, why do we feel a label is so important? Will this label continue to help or hinder Jon in his daily life?

Chapter Two

What do I tell people about autism?

> Where there is much desire to learn, there of necessity will be much arguing, much writing, many opinions; for opinion in good men is but knowledge in the making.
>
> *(Milton 1644, from Areopagitaca)*

What do I know about autism?

I write the following because this is one conversation I have with people all the time. I may not always have the opportunity to go into detail, so they may get an abbreviated explanation, but this is what *I* tell others about my son's disability and how *I* try to explain. Your explanation may be different from mine, but invariably we are all asked the same questions at one time or another.

How common is autism?

The US Centers for Disease Control and Prevention have released their first national estimate of the prevalence of autism in the USA today. They have found that approximately one in every 185 schoolchildren are on the autism spectrum.

What is a spectrum?

Autism spectrum, to me, means a rainbow. A child may be autistic, but will be placed anywhere on that rainbow, and no two children are placed in exactly the same spot. Autism is definitely an *individual* disability.

If this disability is based on individuality, how do they come up with a diagnosis?

After almost 50 years of research, since Kanner first studied a group of children he called autistic, there are now specific criteria, listed in the DSM-IV (*Diagnostic and Statistical Manual*) and the ICD-10 (*International Classification of Disease*). Both state that the child be impaired in at least three of the following developmental areas:

- impairments in social interaction
- impairments in communication
- repetitive or stereotyped patterns of behavior or impairment in functional/symbolic play.

If my child displays impairments in all three of these areas and is diagnosed along the autism spectrum, will this always be so? Will there ever be a change?

Jon has changed greatly since being diagnosed almost ten years ago. Things that once caused him to have autistic moments no longer do so. However, there are new issues daily. Now, different things cause autistic moments. So yes, my son has changed, but the autism is still there. Behaviors change, the fact of autism doesn't.

When Jon was diagnosed, one of the educators told us that after eight years had passed, we could destroy, or expunge, school records. Would this be a beneficial thing to do?

I have often wondered about this. We were told that we could get rid of past school records after eight years. In a heartbeat, this label of autism will be gone. Should we do this? Should we take away all obvious supports for Jon and let him into the real world without autism following him around? I am aware that other parents have done so. Once their high-functioning individual grew closer to college and adulthood, they withdrew the school records because they wanted their child to live free of this label. I'm not sure how this works in the UK or other school systems, but in the US it seems that this is an option. I have also heard young adults speak about this themselves, where they decided not to disclose their disability in an effort to try to live label-free.

Does this work? Would this work in Jon's case? Once again, a very individual issue. What has kept me from doing so up to this point, is that Jon has always had an aide with him in the regular classroom, which has allowed him to attend every class with his peers and stay in the regular curriculum. I feel that first we need to get away from having an aide, and teach him to be more independent in High School. Later, maybe he can go to college or into the workforce without carrying his label along with him.

I also had a counselor tell me that no matter how high functioning Jon becomes or appears to be to us, and others, his autism will not magically disappear. Why would we *not* want to give Jon any support he may need to go to college? Or any support in the workforce? To me, it would be like sending a sightless person to college or work, without the support of their cane or a Braille writer. This person is doing well, why take away any supports they may need?

Then, after thinking all of this through, I notice Jon is doing great. If we didn't explain his autism to others, they may assume he is just an introvert who happens to be a little quirky. When I taught at college, didn't I have several students, without IEPs, who fit this same description? Could it be that they left their label behind them in High School, before coming to college?

Alas, another issue that puts me on the fence.

Will my child be able to go off to college like other kids their age?

Jon talks constantly about attending college—somewhere. But in the same breath he says he wants to live at home and go to college, because he has no desire to experience dorm life. Perhaps he has heard negative things about college dorms? He is only in his second year at High School, so now we tell him, "You can do anything you want to try to do." But some of it, we realize, he may not be able to do. Medical school? (No interest there because of the blood and guts.) Become a firefighter? (Not too sure if he would make the cut physically.) Be the director of an orchestra? (He is in love with this idea, but not with the fact that he would have to learn to play several musical instruments.)

Thus while trying to encourage him, we are trying to help him face the reality of life too. I've been explaining to him recently that most famous people have had to have talent also. That the person directing the orchestra had a talent for music, which they then developed. The singer had a musical voice they developed. Jon has a talent for drawing that we are hoping to develop because he is interested in computer animation.

I explain this to him, and he tells me, "Okay, I get it." Then a few days later I overhear him telling someone, "I want to be a band or orchestra director, but I don't know how to play any instruments. But I *wanted* to play one." Invariably this person then asks me something like, "Why can't he learn to play an instrument?" And I have to explain to them, and to Jon all over again that the reality of such a job is based on talent. Jon has never played an instrument other than the recorder in fourth grade choir. He hasn't shown a talent for music. How could he become a director without musical talent? Maybe I should just quit trying to explain and sign him up for private music lessons? It's a difficult call.

Will my child ever get married? Have a family?

Jon talks about finding a girlfriend. He says he will never have kids because he can't stand babies crying. Over the years I have seen several autistic adults get married, divorced, remarried. I believe this question is the most individual of all, and very similar to neurotypical adults. These days there is not a 100 percent guarantee that a normal person will marry and have a family. In fact there are many happy people living in the world who are single, and who are married, without any desire of having children. I believe when Jon reaches an age, he will have these options too. He can live alone, or live with someone. He can get married, have children or not have children. All of the options are there for him too.

A million dollar question? What do I think caused my son's autism?

I used to assume it was I, the mom, who made my son autistic. Then I read up on the history of autism, about what we know now, that we didn't know then. I realize a parent, a mom, can't *cause* autism. The cause of autism is a very controversial question, one that is ongoing. They are still studying childhood vaccines to see if there is any connection at all, and they continue to look into environmental factors. I believe neither of these two have proven to be the cause of Jon's autism. We know how the brain develops, we know how the wires connect, we just don't know what caused Jon's wires to connect differently. They are saying it is most likely genetic, similar to the findings of Down Syndrome and other disabilities. It was the combination of my genes and my husband's, which produced Jon, and thus produced his autism. So, at this moment in time, they do not have the definitive answer.

Does this bother me that I don't know what caused his autism? Sometimes. When I'm having a conversation, very similar to the one in this chapter, this question comes up. Up to this point, I've had answers, and of course opinions, to all of their questions, but when this one shows up, all I can do is relate what the experts say and what they are doing to try to find a cause. (Then of course, I can give my personal-non-professional-mom's opinion.)

I think it is probably genetics. My husband remembers having a "strange" cousin when growing up who had something "up" with him. I have a cousin who could probably carry the diagnosis of Rett's Syndrome (affects mostly females and is on the spectrum). But because she is about my age, I don't believe this official diagnosis was ever given to her. Rett's is genetic; my husband had something on his side too. My *personal* conclusion—autism is in our family's genetic makeup.

Is it important for me to know what causes autism?—No. It won't change my son's life. Of course it will greatly benefit other parents, and future children. But knowing what caused it probably won't get rid of it in our lives.

Would you get rid of this autism if you had the opportunity?

Another controversial question. Defeat Autism Now (DAN) is a large organization whose purpose is in their name. They want to erase, eradicate, get rid of, and fix autism. But I've read articles by several adults who say that if you take away their autism, you take away an important part of themselves. This is their persona. They are a person first and foremost, but autism is so wrapped up in who they are, that if you get rid of the autism you would in effect wipe out the person.

Of course I see and understand where they are coming from. Yet I still believe autism is a disability. It is something that hinders my son's life. It may also affect him in positive ways, as in giving him an amazing ability to memorize things. But who in their right mind would wish to have autism just to have an amazing memory? Jon will probably never become a rebel, go off and join a gang or do drugs, because his autism keeps him socially disabled and attached to his parents. But what parent would wish their child had such a disability to keep them out of trouble?

I will always remember the first person, bless her, who told me that God knew my husband and I could handle the gift of an autistic child, so he gave us Jon. I didn't say much to her at that moment but later I told my husband, "A gift? Well excuse me, I don't think this is a gift and if it is, I'm giving it back!" I personally have a strong faith in God, but I believe autism showed up and God is helping me get through it. I don't believe my God gifted me, or Jon, with it. So, yes, if I found out tomorrow that something out there would take away Jon's autism, wild horses couldn't hold me back from lining up, with Jon in tow.

What else?

When it comes right down to it, when all is said and done, I try to listen to a twelfth-century philosopher, Maimonides who said: "Teach thy tongue to say 'I do not know.'" Life is really a verb, not a noun, in my mind. It is ongoing, changing, and never the same. Jon's autism is a verb too. In the end I need to say "I don't know…yet."

Is it true that you only really achieve true knowledge once you realize that you don't know?

What do we do with the good intentions of others?

Hell is paved with good intentions.

(English proverb)

As I was growing up, one of my dad's favorite stories was about a man who came to his married couples Sunday School class. Dad was a self-made philosopher and for a few years volunteered to teach an adult class. He told the story that during one session a young man's attitude was to constantly question, argue, or disagree with everything, just for disruption's sake. Dad related that one day, he finally got this man to cease his constant arguing by telling him, "You know, Mike. Everyone has a purpose in this life. And even if your purpose in this class is to give us a bad example, you are serving your purpose." He said from that day on, Mike stopped arguing for argument's sake and actually began to contribute to the class productively. Dad added this to his life's philosophy: if someone's only purpose in life was to give us a bad example, this then was their purpose.

I begin this chapter with Dad's philosophy because mixed in with his world-view was his advice not to get upset over what a person does if their intent was good. If I had a nickel for every time he told me this, I would be a very wealthy woman.

But at the ripe old age of 40-something, in dealing with the way others deal with my son, I seriously ask, "What do we do with good intentions?" Do we take them all to heart? Listen to their advice? Must we always believe they are good? That they mean well?

My first thought goes back to when my son was two and a half. We were living in California at the time, not yet having moved back to the mid-west. Jon was a typical child as far as we knew, meeting most of his developmental goals, perhaps just a little delayed in speech because (we were told) we were a bilingual family. One evening after fighting the rush hour traffic to pick Jon up from his new daycare, I was almost home before I realized that we had left his binky (pacifier) at the center. Rather than drive all the way back to get it, I pulled off at the corner grocery store. After picking up a few items, I was in the checkout line with two binkys (better to be safe, he may not like one of them), when the young checker stopped checking my items and looked up. "Don't you think that guy is a little old for these?" he asked. My mouth dropped open in surprise and I quickly looked the young man over; jeans, shaggy hair, 19 years old, tops. I closed my mouth on the ugly comment I had been about to make and replied to this young person, who probably didn't have a two-and-a-half-year-old, "Whatever makes him happy!"

Good intentions? He probably meant well, my dad would say.

Me? I just blew his question off, as coming from someone who was totally clueless and not worth the effort in coming up with a better response.

Flash forward to after our move back to the mid-west, the summer my son was in a church pre-school program, before attending kindergarten in the fall. No diagnosis yet, but we had noticed he didn't like loud noises, he sang or talked to himself a lot, and could repeat the words from his favorite video, verbatim. He also threw fantastic fits sometimes and would lie on the floor like a log, face down, if he didn't like something. I got a call from a woman who identified herself as the director for the "Parents as Teachers Program." She said she was working with the schools on the new students who would be entering kindergarten in the fall and during this process had contacted the children's preschool teachers, if applicable. She had spoken to Jon's teacher, who had shared some concerns about my son. Would I be interested in stopping by to see the report?

Does a fish take to water? Of course I was interested, and I left work early to get to her office before she closed for the day.

Imagine my surprise when I sat down and read his teacher's comments. For the first time I saw in writing that a teacher was having difficulty working with my son and that she thought he had some serious issues going on. She said he often talked to himself, not to others, and was not yet playing with any other children. He became extremely upset over small issues, like getting water on himself at the drinking fountain, and was able to lie on the floor for long periods of time as if he were comatose. It was in this report where I read the words for the first time "autistic like." It was at that point I stopped reading, and handed the report back to her.

"Thank you," I said. "But this teacher is really wrong here." I then proceeded to explain to her why Jon didn't like to get water on himself (finicky), why he talked to himself (because he was acting out those videos in his head), and why he had developed the habit of lying on the floor face down (tantrum). I thanked her again for calling me, and the next day, instead of dropping Jon off at the preschool I went in to tell the teacher that he would no longer be attending. I also told her that she obviously hadn't listened when I had explained about Jon's finicky behavior, or that our family was bilingual, and that he was slow to speak because of this. And as for her other comments, I told her she needed to be careful what terms she flung around so carelessly, which upset me very much, and possibly other parents!

Did she have good intentions? I'm sure she did. And of course we now know that she was right. But don't worry; we live in a small town and what goes around generally does come back around. Several years later, when Jon was in second grade, whom did the school hire as a special education teacher? This same teacher. She had finished a degree in special education and was Jon's case manager for the latter part of the year, coming in at January. By this time we not only had a diagnosis, and accepted it, we were in the process of reading, studying, and becoming the experts in our son's care. Needless to say, she saw a very different parent from the one of two years before.

Later, after this woman had been introduced to us at our IEP meeting, I told my husband, "See, God either has a sense of humor or he's giving me a chance to let this lady know, one, she was right, and two, I don't hold a grudge against her for trying to drop this bombshell on me two years ago." My husband, bless him, said it was both.

Soon I was able to tell this woman I had been wrong, and to hear her say, "I meant well," her exact words.

A few years later, someone else's good intentions were inflicted on us, and I do mean inflicted. That fall I had been asked to write an editorial from a parent's perspective for a newspaper about 40 miles north of our town. I was friends with a journalist who was writing a series of articles on the school system and special education. My comments about the difficulties in getting necessary services, for our autistic son, and continuing to get them, ran side by side next to an interview with the superintendent of schools, who commented about the need to cut back services for "these types" of kids because they will possibly "drain the coffers."

After this article was published, front page, weekend section, my husband was attending a local real estate meeting. He was in the middle of mingling when a total stranger walked up to him. She interrupted him and said, "I read your wife's article and I feel so sorry for your family and what you must be going through to raise your autistic child!"

My husband said his mouth dropped open and he was at a complete loss for words. But not to worry, because this lady waxed eloquent. She went on to say that she just thought it was terrible that the schools were thinking of cutting the budget for these types of kids and how did our family handle all of the stress not to mention financial issues? My husband managed to close his mouth, take a deep breath, and told her "excuse me," as he quickly moved away.

Later, when he was relating this experience to me, he said he had been so embarrassed and caught off guard. First of all, this was a total stranger, coming up to him in the middle of a business meeting. Second, we certainly didn't need her to feel *sorry* for us, or *pity* us because our son is autistic. And third, he told me never to write under my real name again. "This town is just too small!" he exclaimed, and I had to agree.

Yes, I can hear my dad say, "This lady only had good intentions." But good grief! Didn't she even stop to think where she was, or how her words or pity would sound to a total stranger? I think not.

Nevertheless, during the last few years, there has always been someone like this lady, or even a teacher working with Jon, who seems to be totally clueless in what she or he, says to, or about, our son. I'm learning to listen, trying to take the good, and ignore the bad.

Do I now believe my dad's philosophy, that most people have good intentions? Maybe, but I admit, I probably interpret the proverb, *The road to hell is paved with good intentions* a little differently. It is supposed to mean that one can have all the good intentions in the world, but if not carried out, they will still end up in hell. To me, however, it means that thoughtless people who use the excuse of good intentions to mask thoughtless deeds, know for sure where they will end up!

Although, according to my dad, these people may have served their purpose by being a bad example in this life, maybe they will also have a miserable time in eternity for what they have done all in the guise of good intentions. I wonder now if Dad ever had difficulty forgiving those good intentions, or is it just me?

Chapter Three
IEPs and those elusive goals

Love our principle, order our foundation, progress our goal.
(Auguste Comte, nineteenth-century philosopher)

Can happiness really be an IEP goal?

When Jon was diagnosed and we were forced into the world of disability, this world included several things, among them a new item called an IEP (Individualized Education Plan). Some districts refer to these as ARDs (Admit, Review and Dismiss), and I'm sure the terms vary all over the world. On my better days I call them IEPs, on my bad, I call them a pain in the neck.

What they basically boil down to is a document that plans out your child's future for the next several years. When I discovered I was part of a team that had to create such an important document, I quickly learned that I needed to do some homework about IEPs so I could intelligently participate.

Ten years ago, I found a minuscule amount of information on putting together an IEP, whereas today, if you go to the internet and type in just the letters IEP you get almost 12 million hits, many of them giving you a definition. Type in "writing IEPs" and you get over 450 thousand places where you can find the words "writing IEPs."

What's a parent to do?

Take heart and try to narrow it down a little. My local library had 14 books listed on this topic, only two published since the year 2000. Online, on Amazon.com, they also had a different 14, only a handful published recently. I suggest finding a book published as recently as possible, or an organization you can trust to give you sound advice. Remember that the Disability Act and subsequent laws protecting your child and enabling him or her to enjoy a free and appropriate education have changed several times since 2000. If you are writing an IEP you want to make sure you are up to date.

Taking all of this into consideration, where does one start?

When we wrote our first IEP we started with thinking about goals. I remember writing at the top of the page, *Our first goal for Jon is to be happy.* Simple yes, but at the time it was where my husband and I needed to start—Jon's happiness, not ours.

At the time, this meant that if he was shutting down every day when he had to go to the music room and take part in music class, instead of just making him "put up with it," we looked into it as an IEP team and considered certain alternatives for him. Along with Jon's autism came hypersensitive hearing. Obviously there was something going on in music class that he could not deal with. So written into his IEP were the options of allowing him to leave the class, with his aide, if things got too much for him, or allowing him to sit somewhere else in the room; that is, further away from the piano, not next to the speakers on the player. Also, at this time, we purchased muffling earphones for him, the type used at shooting ranges. He was allowed to wear these when he wanted to, and as a result was able to sit in music class.

We began his IEP with the goal of happiness, but we were able to break it down from there into particulars of what happiness for him might mean, at that moment in time.

Next, I learned to make all IEP goals *measurable.* So, if we look at the goal above, relating to Jon's happiness and his obvious unhappiness during music class, the goal was written something along the lines of "Jon would be able to sit through music class four out of six times" and "would develop a different response to the stress of the class, other than shutting down, four out of six times." This made the educators happy; this was something that lined up with the laws of having something to count, something measurable, and this made us happy in that we were working towards the goal of Jon's happiness during music class.

Of course since that first IEP, Jon's needs and goals have changed. In getting ready for his first year of High School, one of the goals was "Jon will appropriately ask peers in the room for help/assistance instead of his aide or the teacher, six out of ten times" and "Jon will take part in group class discussion, without prompting, eight out of ten times." I anticipate that, as we try to work the aide out of the classroom and out of Jon's life, there will be more and more similar goals like this one.

After working on IEPs for over ten years, do I just whip them out of my head and they become "law"?—Not hardly. Each year, as we get close to our annual review or twice-yearly IEP writing, I still get on the internet and look through the hundreds of websites on how to write an IEP, along with sample IEPs. Not only because the IDEA (Individuals with Disabilities Education Act) laws have been changing, but also because I usually find something someone else has written into an IEP that I may not have thought of.

There is a wonderful site at www.spedforms.com published by the special education department in Pipestone, Minnesota. Not only do they have several specific pages under "Developing IEP Goals," they also have "The Stranger Test & the Dead Man's Test." This is one I had not heard of before.

The Stranger Test means to write goals for the student so if a stranger who has never worked with the student reads them, they would understand the goal. An example of this would be a goal we had for Jon at one time, which was to not use violence in response to kids picking on him, but to learn to react with language. If a teacher read this who was a stranger to Jon, they would read *violence*, and think rages? fighting? throwing things? Whereas what we specifically meant was, pushing the students away, a shove, a punch in the arm, all things that Jon had done and needed to learn to do differently. The better goal would have been to list these specifics in the goal, so that even a stranger would understand it.

The Dead Man's Test means to answer the question, can a dead man do it? If a dead man can do it, it is not an appropriate goal. Again in Jon's case if the goal is to get him not to be rude to teachers or adults and we write "not rude to teachers or adults" as the target goal, this will not pass. A dead man could meet this goal and not be rude to teachers or adults. A better goal would be "speaks to teachers and adults in a polite manner," listing examples of what this would mean. This passes, because a dead man can't speak and meet this goal.

Perhaps these two tests have been around a long time in special education circles, if only I would have found them sooner, it would have made goal writing much clearer.

Another place I have always found very helpful, specific, IEP information is at www.udel.edu.bkirby/asperger/, the OASIS (Online Asperger Syndrome Information and Support) web page. Not only do they have pages of IEP goals and checklists, but several of their forms are similar to "fill-ins" where a parent can print them out and fill in their own child's information, and take them to the next IEP meeting.

I also found linked to the site Wrightslaw.com (where you can find everything you need to know about your rights) a humorous look at IEPs, written by Aimee Gilman. To all parents who have wanted to run kicking and screaming from an IEP meeting, or perhaps wanted to not show up at all, this article is for you. When she writes: "The members of the TEAM will fix their collective glare on you because you had the gall to have this child at all, and look how many people are inconvenienced," I couldn't help but laugh in agreement. Too many times we have seen how inconvenient our IEP, follow-up, or progress meetings are for the educators to attend. My husband and I soon learned to try personally to thank each one of them for taking the time out of their busy schedules to show up. Yes, I know, it's their job. But once again, my husband's salesmanship comes through as he reminds me to play the game, and try to spread a little good feeling along the way. Another one of his mottos also comes to mind "You can't fight City Hall." So? You might as well play the game.

One last place for IEP help would be to go to www.orgsites.com/ md/asperger_syndrome_info. Here you will find a week's worth of sites to link to for information on IEPs.

But to get back to my original question, with all of this knowledge, all of these specifics and checklists, can happiness be an IEP goal?

To this day, in the middle of Jon's High School years, we still place this at the top of all of our IEPs. By now the team members know us and if they are new teachers, they will soon learn that in our case, *Jon's* happiness really is our goal. If Jon wants to plan on going to college, we will help him work towards that goal. If he wants to work as a fast food prep cook we will help him with that one. After visiting another zoo, a rather compulsive interest of his right now, he thinks he may be interested in zoology and working in a zoo. This is very far away from where he has been heading, working in a library and library science, but if this will make him happy, we will try to help him get there.

It is no different from when he was little and was miserable in music class. At that moment in time, we wanted him to be happy, so we worked through it. Now that he is staring young adulthood in the face, we only want the same thing for him.

Happiness *can* be an IEP goal, if you then continue from that point on, and put in place all of the other important elements of a good IEP.

If my child's happiness is the goal, as he grows older, how do I find a balance between practicality and happiness?

chicken nugget #3

Autism and gray

"Is there anything in life that is really black and white?"

(Me, in exasperation)

"A newspaper...no, maybe not. Okay...a zebra!"

(Jon, triumphantly)

When my son was in about fourth grade he walked up to a total stranger on the street, shook his finger at him and said, "Ah, ah, ah! Smoking will kill you!" I quickly apologized to this person, took Jon gently by the arm and after walking some distance away, explained to him that smoking was a freedom that people have.

"But it's bad for you."

"Yes, but this is a choice that person has made, to smoke or not. They are an adult and if they wish to smoke, it is their choice."

"But people who smoke are punks and hoods," he insisted.

"And where did you hear that?"

"At school, you know in the DARE program."

Yes, I did know. The Dare program (Drug Abuse Resistance Education) is a very popular and successful program in our state that tries to educate kids to keep them away from drugs, smoking, and alcohol. Unfortunately, this program was geared toward neurotypical kids, not autistic kids who only see life in black and white, good and bad, no in-between. So when my son attended these classes he came away with the firm conviction and knowledge that all drugs were bad, including smoking and alcohol, and anyone who used any form of drug was a bad person.

How could I explain the subtle differences to him in this antidrug message? I started out by telling him that illegal drugs were bad, and yes, he did not want to be around kids who were doing drugs like uppers or downers, or smoking pot. (I'm sure my terms needed to be brought into the twenty-first century, but he knew what I was talking about!) I told him if he ever saw any of these things, he needed to get as far away from them as possible and find an adult. Then I explained to him that although his DARE officer had referred to alcohol and cigarettes as drugs, these two things were legal and it was the abuse of these two things, drinking too much, smoking too much, which made these items bad. But, the people who smoked or drank alcohol were not breaking any law and were not automatically bad people, or as he had said, punks or hoods. He listened, some of it sunk in. But over the years, it seems like after every yearly DARE officer visit at school, we ended up having this same conversation.

Thus, as he got older, I also tried to explain to him that life was not black and white, good or evil; that there was some gray area in life and that smoking and drinking fell into that gray area. He would listen and nod his head, but I knew we would probably be going through it all again. My son does not see gray.

This fact was brought home after Jon began drawing lessons. He had developed an interest in computer animation, researched the topic on the internet, and found there were several years of basic art and drawing classes required before a student ever gets to a computer animation class. As a result, a friend of ours began tutoring Jon one night a week in basic drawing.

Her patience with Jon was amazing, and I sat and listened to her instructions to Jon as she tried to get him to see the object she wished him to draw. I also got into the habit of taking a book to read so I wouldn't be a "sideline mom" always jumping in, trying to take over the game.

One evening as I was sitting a distance away, I heard her say, "No. Can't you see the gray here? Don't use that dark black there, this shadow has different shading here. See that gray?" I closed my book and watched as Jon tried to draw his vision of the still-life pitcher and fruit they were working on.

"No. Can you see that's too dark?" she said again.

Jon was getting frustrated. "That's what I see."

"Okay. Then let's do this. Let's take the eraser and take some of that black out," she said.

So instead of shading lighter with the black and the white oil crayons, she had him go ahead and use the black, and erase it down to gray shadow.

At the end of the session I stopped her for a private word to explain that one of the traits of Jon's autism is the problem of seeing everything in life as black and white. With Jon, life, or people, are good or evil, black or white. He could not see any gray in life.

She looked at me in surprise. "Well, you are right about that! We can only draw what our brain allows us to see and he can't see gray."

We both thought this was very interesting and during the next sessions, keeping this in mind, she made it a special point to show him where the gray was in what they were drawing. By the end of the three-month session, he was just beginning to be able to see a little bit of gray or lighter black, when he was asked.

Did this translate into his life? Can he see any gray in the world around him? Well, we haven't had any of those talks lately, but recently when he got upset because we couldn't go somewhere, he stated, "Okay, fine! I'll *never* go anywhere *ever* again!" (Arms crossed, angry frown.)

I said, "You know, Jon. Life doesn't always have to be all or nothing, either or. Why don't you walk down the middle of the road instead of going all the way to one side, left or right?"

He laughed. "Middle of the road! That's funny, Mom!"

Yes, it was a funny analogy. But if his art teacher can help him slowly to see gray, maybe I can also help him sometimes to take the middle of the road. Goodness knows, sometimes the middle of the road is the safer path!

Chapter Four

Charting growth

Make up your mind…before it is too late, that the fitting thing for you to do is live as a mature man who is making progress…

(Epictetus)

How can we tell if our child is maturing?

Because of Jon's autism, his maturity level is about two years behind his peers. So, when we had a sixth grader we really had a fourth grader. When he was in Junior High, he was still, maturity-wise, in elementary school. This helps explain why he was trying to decide which Power Ranger toy to get next, when most other eighth graders were trying to decide what type of car they wanted to drive. It also explains why he wanted Disney's *Sleeping Beauty* DVD for his collection over Eddie Murphy's *Daddy Day-Care*.

Does this immaturity really matter? I don't think so, as long as we, and those working with him, understand and try to remember that he will probably always be about two years behind.

So, when a note is sent home reporting that he is calling other students, who are kidding around with him, names like "chicken-brain" and "butt-head" we try not to overreact. We explain to him that even though he thinks these are funny names, he shouldn't be calling anyone any names at all. Then we write a note back to the teacher and explain that we will try to get Jon to interact a little more age-appropriately and stop silly name calling, but, we add, isn't it great that he is socially inter-acting with his peers? There was a time not too long ago when he was completely oblivious to any other students and would go all day without any social interaction. My husband and I think it's great that he is taking part in horse-play and silly name calling.

See, we point out, he *is* maturing!

Which brings me to my point: How can we tell if our children are maturing? I'm not talking about meeting IEP goals, or academic challenges, but maturing the way neurotypical children mature. With Jon, it shows in small ways, such as his delight when he finally learned to snap both fingers, and sometimes in big ways.

About a year ago Jon and I visited a large pizza place together, where the eating areas are divided into 1960s-style dining rooms. Jon and I went alone because he was going to be going there with his classmates on a field trip and if possible, he and I like to visit places beforehand so he will know what to expect. We wandered around, touring the entire area and Jon decided to sit in the retro-60s movie room. We carried our pizza in and sat down to enjoy a movie, which happened to be *The Pink Panther*.

Two notable things happened during this movie, one was that my son actually enjoyed this "older" movie and wanted to stay and watch the entire thing. Two was that he usually requests I take a fork and scrape every single thing off of the pizza until he is down to sauce and crust. (He has this extreme aversion to cheese.) But at this time, it was a little dark, and he was into watching the movie. Instead of scraping everything off the top, I picked off the pieces of pepperoni and handed it back to him. Then I tried not to pay too much attention as he ate it.

I think I held my breath as he suddenly stopped after the first bite and said, "Hmm, this tastes...different, but good." He took another bite. I leaned towards him and explained that I had picked off the pepperoni and he was eating a cheese pizza. Even in the semi-dark I could see his eyes grow big as he tried to look at the piece of pizza in his hand. He took another bite, this one flipped upside down.

"Hmmm... I sorta like it!" His voice showed surprise.

Talk about a monumental moment in the Boushéy family! I went up to the pizza bar and refilled our plates, making sure he had a few more slices of cheese pizza. I sat back down and he and I had a wonderful time watching the bumbling Inspector Clouseau, and eating our pizza.

At the time I didn't make a comment on the fact that he was finally eating a piece of pizza with the topping on, but as soon as I had a moment I called my husband on the cell phone to report what had happened.

"All right!" My husband exclaimed. "With the cheese topping!"

A sign of maturing tastebuds, and for Jon, with autism, this was a major breakthrough.

Another breakthrough was a few summers ago. Jon has always had sleeping problems. When he was little and was out of a crib and into a bed, he would wake up like clockwork between three and four every morning and appear by my side of the bed. When I realized that this was just a ritual with him, and that he was okay, I would pat him on the arm and tell him, go back to sleep, it was too early to get up, and he did.

As he grew older we lived in several different homes and he learned to stay in bed all night, but then the difficulty became *getting* to sleep. So, my husband and I got in the habit of lying down with him until he went to sleep. After his diagnosis in kindergarten we figured that these sleeping problems probably had something to do with autism (although I've only read a few books containing chapters discussing this) and we realized we had to deal with his sleeping problems individually as they came along.

Thus, it was no surprise that soon after he started being able to go to sleep by himself again, he was getting up in the night and coming to stand by the side of the bed. Since he hadn't been doing this since he was little, we were now able to ask him what the problem was. He tried to explain that he just didn't like waking up in the middle of the night and being the only one awake. And he didn't like lying in his bed by himself and trying to go back to sleep. So we devised a plan that if he would wake up in the middle of the night, he could come and lie down on a bed that we made for him on the floor in our bedroom. This not only satisfied him, but he went to sleep easier, knowing that he had an option that if he woke up in the middle of the night, he could come to our room.

This phase went on for a long time. It got to the point that I didn't wake up any more when he crawled into his covers on the floor, and I seriously started considering buying a small futon to fold up and fold down in the corner of our room; much better than the mattress and blankets on the floor.

Then suddenly, after a year or so, he stopped getting up in the middle night and coming into our room. The first few times this happened and I awoke to *not* find him on the floor, I got up to check on him to see if he was all right. Of course he was fine, sleeping soundly in his own bed; and I realized that this phase was over, he was maturing.

He still doesn't like going to sleep at night, but now, after going to bed, he gets back up, brings his pillows with him, lies on the couch for about ten minutes or so, then goes back to bed. This usually happens only once a night, and when we asked him about this, he said he just doesn't like lying there and waiting for sleep, he would rather come lie on the couch until he feels sleepy and then go back to bed.

My husband and I are in agreement, we've come a long way with sleeping problems, and if this works for him, it works for us.

How do I know my son is maturing? Do I have to wait until it leaves the branch? Or in Jon's case, leaves home?

I continue to notice small and big ways. Just this morning I noticed that he is tall enough to put the glasses away out of the dishwasher onto the top shelf of the cabinet. Recently, when I dropped him off at school in the pouring rain, my son, who used to have a severe autistic meltdown if he got wet in the rain, hurried through the rain drops to the front door, turned with a smile, and gave me a thumbs up!

In *Hours in a Library*, Virginia Woolf wrote, "One of the signs of passing youth is the birth of a sense of fellowship with other human beings as we take our place among them." I am looking for this sign in Jon too, no matter that he is autistic.

I think I may have noticed it the other day when he saw, and more importantly, recognized, one of his fellow classmates at the store.

"Hey chicken-breath!" Jon called to him.

Ah yes, he is taking his place among his fellow human beings! He is maturing!

Will he be a few years behind for the rest of his life?

chicken nugget #4

Living with fear

Where the fear is, happiness is not.

(Seneca, Roman philosopher)

What are you afraid of?

I must answer this question, before I can ask it. When Jon was first diagnosed and I was in the midst of reading everything on autism I could get my hands on, I would sometimes sit fearfully, and wait for his symptoms to become worse. Was I told they would become worse? No. But because I was reading up on developmental delays, speech, physical, social, and emotional, I waited for Jon *not* to develop in these areas. Is that a backwards way of thinking for a parent, or what? Like placing your foot on a chair, then reaching down and tying the shoe of the foot that is still resting on the floor.

I was afraid he wouldn't develop speech past his early echolalia. I sat and watched to see if he became more catatonic in his gaze. I was afraid he would exhibit attention deficit disorder along with his autism. Even when he started progressing, after working with physical therapy, occupational therapy, and his speech teacher, I was afraid he would regress and looked for signs that he was going backwards in his development. For a long time I carried this giant load of fears around with me daily. How did I get rid of them?

I remember at one point, sitting in the living room watching Jon watch TV. I must have been sitting and worrying, because suddenly tears started rolling down my cheeks, and in that moment I realized that I could not hover over him and watch for signs of *non*-development or *worse* development. I was becoming neurotic and Jon didn't need that. He needed someone who could look at *him* and not at the autism he happened to have. I got up, explained to him that I was turning the TV off and that we were going to the park. I don't know why, but I felt I needed to do something physical to stop this habit of fear.

When we got to the park he got on his favorite piece of equipment, the swing, and I sat down in the one next to him. He had just learned to pump with his legs and I challenged him to a race to see who could swing higher. As we swung, I mentally tried to name all of the worries that I had been carrying around with me, then as I swung back and forth, I let each worry drop to the ground at my feet and told myself I would not pick them up again.

After a while, Jon got off the swing and went to play on the jungle gym, a great big yellow monstrosity that had slides and ladders connected to it. I sat in my swing and watched him play—not with the other kids, but with himself—and I made myself notice how happy he was. My son, who happened to be autistic, was such a happy camper! He wasn't afraid of running and jumping and crawling over this jungle gym. He seemed to be unafraid of anything, and was happy. While here I was, driving myself crazy with fear. Who was the one with the problem? I vowed to stop.

I left that park and I refused to take those worries home with me. I determined to look at my son and see Jon, only Jon. Not autism.

Obviously this happened a long time ago, but recently it all came flooding back. We were out for a Sunday drive, enjoying the early autumn weather, and my husband commented that he wanted to sit down with me so we could map out a plan to retire in ten years. I nodded my head and mentally figured that Jon would be about 24 by that time. My husband continued talking, I kept on nodding in agreement, but suddenly began to cry.

He glanced over. "What?"

After a few minutes I was able to tell him that I understood he wanted to retire in ten years, and yes, I would go along with everything he planned, but please don't ask me to actually do the planning or "deep" thinking about it. As I continued to cry I tried to explain to him that I could only plan for Jon one year in advance. He would be in High School the next year, and I could only read up, prepare, and plan ahead, this far in his life. My husband didn't really understand, but he agreed.

Later, I realized that this is how I keep the fears away. I read up, study for, and plan ahead, only one year at a time. Anything more than that overwhelms me. Does this mean I'm denying the fact my son will grow to be 24 years of age right about when my husband wants to retire? Of course not. I know he will grow up and possibly grow away from us, or not.

Because of his autism, we don't know what 24 will be like for Jon until Jon gets there. But my fears are suddenly calmed when I realize I don't have to plan for 24 now, I only have to plan for High School. So with my one-year-at-a-time planning, and my husband's far-sighted planning, I have been able to keep the fears of my son's future at bay.

Virginia Woolf wrote through her character Mrs. Dalloway: "Fear no more, says the heart. Fear no more, says the heart, committing its burden to some sea which sighs collectively for all sorrows, and renews, begins, collects, lets fall." Mrs. Dalloway let her fears drop into the peaceful sea, whereas I left mine on that playground.

Now I can ask—what are *you* afraid of? And I can attest to the fact that if we don't put these fears down and refuse to carry them around with us, we may drive ourselves over the edge. Some use prayer, some seek counseling; use whatever works for you, but do drop them and don't pick them up again.

It was also about this time that my ever-practical husband made an appointment with our attorney. Yes, I went, not quite kicking and screaming, to his office and after about an hour's interview, we had him set up a living trust to plan for Jon's future. This resulted in a detailed discussion of possible guardianship and conservatorship. But thanks to my husband, who *can* look that far into the future, we now have something very solid in place.

And now that my fears are allayed, what should I do with the part of my brain which constantly worried?

Chapter Five

Understanding Jon's way of understanding

Or, *Lost in Translation* is not just a movie title

I didn't know I had to know that.

(Jon, eighth grade)

My son has a learning difference, but *how* does he learn?

The above quote may sound redundant, but since I am Jon's mom, I know exactly what he means by this. This means, yes, he was paying attention, yes, he was aware of the information being given to him, but he didn't know he was going to be responsible for remembering or understanding it. It didn't click with him, and he didn't study or memorize the information. As a result, he was unable to pass a test, or a quiz; and when this happens, he gets upset and says, "I knew the information but I didn't know I had to know it!"

Makes perfect sense to me. I know important directions were given to Jon, but they were probably given so the class as a whole, neurotypical students could pick them up, not a student like Jon with learning differences. As a result, the instructions were what I call *lost in translation*.

When Jon was first diagnosed high-functioning autistic, I found it necessary to try to simplify an explanation of his learning differences for teachers, and others, who would come into contact with him. I would explain that Jon's brain developed neurologically differently, resulting in developmental delays, which then resulted in learning differences (my choice of word over *disabilities*). Sometimes I needed to explain all of this in a nutshell, so they could understand Jon without actually understanding every aspect of autism. As a result, I compared Jon's brain to a computer.

I would explain that his brain is very similar to a computer and a computer's hard drive. If the information is not put onto the hard drive, it will not be running on the computer. Similarly, if Jon is not given specific instructions along with information, this information may not be written on his hard drive. For example, he will not know that the handout that was passed out needs to be read, understood and perhaps memorized later for a quiz, unless he is *told* all of the above. And don't tell him all of the above all at once either. Break it down in simple steps for him: 1. Read the handout. 2. Make sure you understand it. 3. Friday we will have a quiz over the information on the handout. 4. Take handout home and review it Thursday night.

And don't give him these directions orally. One of my son's major learning differences is he has great difficulty with auditory learning. Be specific, break it down into simple instructions and write it down, or better yet, have him write it down. If you've done this, the information will be written on his hard drive. Keeping to the computer analogy, I also would explain that although his brain is similar to a computer's hard drive and his memory is amazing, his processing speed is still running at XT speed in a Pentium world. Therefore, please realize that he will get the information he is being given, but give him extra time to process and respond to it

This nutshell explanation worked for a long time, and then I changed it. As Jon matured, I began explaining to people that Jon has "autistic moments." Because he is *high*-functioning autistic, he may be blending in, going with the flow, when something may upset him, stress him out, or set him off. This is when he has an autistic moment. These moments used to be head banging (his own head with his fist, not someone else's), fist pounding on a desk or wall, and, when he is really upset, tears. But as he's grown older we've tried to redirect these moments so he can learn to react differently. Some of these upsets haven't stopped, but he is trying. Instead of tears he does a lot of gulping and takes deep breaths. To try to get away from head banging he is learning to clutch his hands into fists and close his eyes until whatever he is feeling has passed. And to keep from overreacting to certain kids at school who know how to "push his buttons" he is learning to joke with them and laugh at them. (Not that I'm not a hawk when it comes to watching out for bullying, but my husband and I have realized that not every kid who picks on him can be stopped. It's a good idea to try to get Jon to learn to deal with it and then we can watch out for any serious problems.)

Most people learn that we don't know when Jon's autistic moments will occur or what will cause them, we just know he will always have them.

Both of these explanations have helped people working with Jon, and in eighth grade I needed to add another explanation—*lost in translation*. Anyone who has learned a foreign language can easily relate. Lost in translation means the real meaning of the sentence, word, expression, or thought is simply lost when translated. Yes, there is communication going on because the person hears and understands the language, but the layered meaning is not getting through. There are many reasons for this, one being that a lot of the meaning in language is built into the culture. If the person learning or listening to that language hasn't experienced the culture behind the language, meaning is lost. It took my husband almost 30 years of living in the United States to understand the line, "I don't think we are in Kansas any more!" (Dorothy says this to Toto when they land in Oz, i.e. we are definitely someplace different than home.) What is funny is that, although Jon is autistic, he was raised on *The Wizard of Oz*, so he easily got this one!

But when it comes to neurotypical teaching in the classroom, to Jon, this is very similar to a foreign language. He will not pick up meaning through inference, or even if he is taking part in the classroom discussion. He doesn't have the cultural background of a neurotypical student to realize that when the teacher writes a list of words on the board, they are important, copy them down.

Jon's culture is not an "osmosis" culture. (Ah ha! Another nutshell.) Osmosis means a gradual almost unconscious process of assimilation. In Jon's case, nothing in his life was, or is unconscious. He learned to speak by echolalia—imitating speech and phrases that he heard on TV, videos, and from others around him. He learned social interaction by practicing scripts with his first speech teacher. He learned what to expect in specific situations by reading "social stories" that his teacher's aide, and I, wrote for him. He is learning in the regular classroom through specific instruction, re-teaching if necessary of any concepts, and written-visual-direction. There is nothing osmosis in any of that, and therefore a lot of what happens around him that neurotypicals pick up, gets lost in translation from their culture to his.

This became extremely evident when in eighth grade Jon wanted to take Spanish. He is fascinated with foreign languages, and with his excellent memory holds hundreds of words and phrases in his head from Japanese to Persian. Thus, we thought this would be great for him, a chance for him to use his memory skills and excel in something he enjoys learning. But we had a slight surprise ahead of us.

Less than two months into the school year we learned that Jon was getting Cs and Ds in Spanish. This, from a normally B and A student, would come as a surprise to any parent. So we scheduled a meeting with a few members of his IEP team and his Spanish teacher. The teacher explained that Jon was failing in conversation skills and test taking. Yes, his memory was amazing, but she felt that learning a language was more than memorization skills, and she specifically geared her quizzes and tests to try to see if the student was really getting the language as a whole. She just didn't think Jon was able to grasp a foreign language, but because he so enjoyed it, she would allow him to stay in the class in hopes that he could still pass it, even with a low grade.

After this meeting I was like a dog with a bone. When someone tells me Jon may not be able to do something, I like to look into it to see if there is a way that we can help him do it, but differently.

Within a few days I found a paper online at ERIC (the Education Resource Information database) titled "A Policy of Inclusions: Alternative Foreign Language Curriculum for High-Risk and Learning Disabled Students" (Pritikin 1999). UK writer Lorin Pritikin points out that with our children's great capacities to memorize, it was not only possible but beneficial to teach them a foreign language. Using French as the language, she lists step by step how she got her students to do this successfully. I would recommend any parent who is struggling with their child and a foreign language class to find this paper, print it out and pass a copy on to the teacher.

The bottom line was Pritikin took advantage of her students' excellent memory skills, and realizing that because they had problems communicating in English, they would also have difficulty communicating in French, she *gave* them communication. She had them all create a phrase book where they pasted or wrote phrases. This became their bible and they were able to memorize from it and communicate with it. She also pointed out that too much information is an overload to these students, and she broke things down and tested them over smaller chunks (Pritikin 1999).

I was delighted to find this article and after printing it, we stopped by to see the Spanish teacher. We gave her a copy of this paper and talked about how it would be possible to teach Jon Spanish *differently*. She seemed somewhat surprised by our visit, and by the information, but she did say she would read it and see what she could do.

Why is it some people think they know better, no matter what? As you can guess by this question, our meeting with the Spanish teacher didn't improve the situation. Jon struggled with this class and we struggled with this teacher the entire school year. We got him a Spanish tutor to work with him twice a week after school, and this is really what kept him going. The teacher seemed to ignore everything in this article and every suggestion we made to try to teach Jon differently. Yes, his para-professional aide and his tutor helped him create a phrase book, but he was not allowed to use it or refer to it during class or test taking. He could only use it to study from. And when she tested him, not only was the test not broken down into small chunks for him, but the phrases were different, reversed, or backwards from the ones he had memorized.

Once we realized the teacher was not using any of the suggestions from the article, or any that we made, we talked about going to the principal to see if he could effect a change. But at the same time we had a major problem with bullying, and decided we could really only fight one battle at a time. Thus, we let the Spanish teacher ignore our advice and went after the bullying issue.

Jon continued to get Cs on his work, and we used this opportunity instead, to teach him that he couldn't be a perfect "A" student, and that there was nothing wrong with a "C" if he had done his best work. By the end of the school year he still had that C, along with all of his As and two Bs, but thankfully it didn't keep him from making the Honor Roll a second year in a row.

In addition, I now tell others who are working with Jon that he is not an "osmosis learner." He will not get what neurotypical students get from just sitting in the classroom. Every other teacher in every other subject worked with this by using handouts, study guides, and even helping him with note taking. It was just this one lone Spanish teacher who refused to teach him differently because she felt that learning Spanish was, how did she put it? "not only memorization but students being able to *ingest* and *embrace* the Spanish language." Funny how those two words right there would not work well with my autistic son. Jon seldom ingests anything without caution because of issues with food smells and textures, and being autistic he really only embraces me, Dad, or a close family member. I wished the teacher could have changed her thinking to: "In this case, memorization is acceptable. In addition, let's feed this language to Jon in small portions so that he may grow comfortable with the language." Just those two slight changes in thinking may have helped my son stay with it and not get so lost.

Next year I will explain to his teachers, and his Spanish II teacher in particular, that this is my son in a nutshell: his brain is like the hard drive on a computer, although still at XT speed; he will continue to have autistic moments, which can't always be predicted; and in the classroom, a lot of what students get by osmosis, he will not.

When Jon tells me, "Mom, I knew that, I just didn't know I was supposed to know it!" there is nothing lost in translation for me. I've been living in his culture for a long time.

How do I make sure others learn more about his culture so that there are no translation problems in the future?

Have I gone over the fence and now believe that autism should be viewed and treated as a culture, not as a disability?

chicken nugget #5

"Sometimes it's all Greek to me too!"—explaining terminology

Have you ever noticed that beneath every culture is a subculture? And this subculture even has its own its own language? So, what does it all mean?

Answers to some of the following can be found in several places on the internet. I found mine in an article entitled "Special Education Jargon in Plain English" at www.geocities.com/Enchanted Forest/Glade/6190/spedjargon.html. by "Heather", a parent/teacher. You can also find a lot of these explanations at the Autism Society of America's website (www.autismsociety.org). Here are a few questions I've had over the years, and some of the answers I've found and adapted from the above spedjargon website (Heather 2004).

Is Section 504 the same as a Section 8, which was what Klinger wanted in the TV series *M*A*S*H*?

No. Although dealing with a Section 504 might drive one nearer to a Section 8 (mental instability). Section 504 is a federal law stating it is illegal to deny participation in activities, benefits, or programs, or to discriminate in any way against a person with a disability solely because of the disability. Individuals with disabilities must have equal access to programs and services. Also, auxiliary aid must be provided to individuals with impaired speaking, manual, or sensory skills.

This is the law in black and white. Of course we realize it is up to individuals to interpret and implement this law in relation to your child. This is why my son has always been allowed a professional aide in our school district and 45 miles up the road he would not have been allowed one, because the law is being interpreted and implemented differently.

Why is PL 94-142 sometimes referred to as the most important law in the history of disabilities?

You may not have liked or voted for President Gerald Ford, but back in 1975 he literally set our disabled children free by signing into law the Education of All Handicapped Children Act. This Public Law 94-142 states that special needs children have the right to free and appropriate public education in the least restrictive environment. This was a major step towards civil rights for children with special needs.

Thank you, Mr. Ford. Because of you, my son, after receiving a diagnosis of high-functioning autism, was not pulled out of the regular classroom and placed into a small special education classroom with severely disabled children. Because of you, the school must work to accommodate my son in the *least restrictive* (love that phrase!) environment, which for him, is the regular classroom. And because of you, my son has prospered in the public schools.

I was told that as a parent, I needed to exercise my child's right to a FAPE in an LRE and to have this written into his/her IEP. What does all of this mean exactly?

Don't let all of the jargon scare you off. This is telling you that your child is entitled to a free and appropriate public education (FAPE) in a least restrictive environment (LRE) and that you need to have this (environment) written into his or her Individualized Education Plan (IEP). This IEP is your child's bible for the school year. This plan is written and drawn up by you and the educators who will be working with your child during the year.

I found out much later after Jon's diagnosis that this plan should not be written before the IEP meeting and brought for the parents to sign. It should be written during the meeting with the parent's full involvement. Included in an IEP are goals, objectives for behavior, and academic achievement, and ways these will be met and measured.

Do I really need to know what PL 99-457 or PL 101-336 are?

Yes and no. Both are public laws and affect your family only if you have an infant or preschool-age child. The first PL 99-457 extended the civil rights of special needs children to include infants and preschool-age children. This law mandated PL 101-336 or IFSP, (Individual Family Service Plan). This plan is similar to an IEP for the school-aged child, stating the child's present levels of skills, but also stating the family's strengths and needs for enhancing the child's development. Goals are set, intervention services scheduled, and project dates for beginning these services. It also helps the child transition into a preschool program.

In February 2005 NBC stations ran a week-long series on autism—what it is, its symptoms and treatments. The main message on every show was that researchers and scientists are now pushing for earlier diagnosis, like at six months, in hopes of having greater success for earlier interventions. In the February 28 2005 issue of *Newsweek* there was an excellent article titled "Babies and autism: Why new research on infants may hold the key to better treatment."

Therefore, knowing what we know now, early treatment is the first place all parents should start after getting as early a diagnosis as possible. If you don't get with your local Disabilities Board and get a written IFSP you may be lost in a maze of services. Some communities, such as mine, have a "Parents as Teachers" program. This is a state-funded program, and the best place to go to get connected for services for a preschool-age child. If your doctor has given you a diagnosis of autism or Asperger's Syndrome for your preschool-age child, they should be able to connect you with an office to help you set up your own IFSP.

Someone mentioned to me that because of the ADA they have to build a ramp into their store. What is that?

They are right. The Americans with Disabilities Act (ADA), and PL 101-336, mandates that no person of any age shall be discriminated against in the areas of transportation, public access, local government, or telecommunications. We now have wheelchair-accessible bathrooms, access ramps, a TDD phone system, and closed captioning for the hearing impaired.

My son thinks closed caption is so cool. He can watch shows with the sound muted! Of course he also changes the TV language to Spanish because he likes to hear his favorite cartoons in a different language. Many a time you can hear me or my husband call out, "Jon! Could you come and show us again how to change the language back to English and turn off the captions?"

Why was I told by an educator that PL 101-476, or IDEA, was the most important law affecting my child?

Because it really is. The Individuals with Disabilities Education Act (IDEA) added another addition to the Education of All Handicapped Children Act that President Ford signed. It changed the "label" for people with special needs from, handicapped to disabled, mandated that transition plans must be implemented for children 16 years or older who receive special services, and (this is the big one), added traumatic brain injury and autism to the list of disabilities that the original law protects.

I wonder now, if IDEA had not been added to the original law, would my son have to fight for every little service because autism would not be listed as a protected disability?

Must I memorize all of these laws and acts?

Memorize? No. But now you are aware, so that when someone uses any of this jargon, you can nod your head, knowing that you read about them. Later if you have to, you can always go back and look it up. Jargon is sometimes a way in which educators unknowingly, or at times knowingly, separate themselves from parents, creating a "we vs. they" attitude. Next time you go into your IEP meeting, if you slip in some jargon at appropriate moments, you will surely take the wind out of their sails when they realize that you too are up on the laws and acts which affect your child. For readers in other countries, yes, you too have your own laws and jargon, which I am unaware of, as we live in the US. But take the time to learn it and use it. And who knows? Maybe they will listen to you a little more closely when you speak.

Remember what writer Oliver Wendell Holmes said, "Man's [or woman's] mind stretched to a new idea never goes back to its original dimensions" (cited in Weinstein 2006). Consider yourself stretched!

Chapter Six

What to take on vacation

How does one travel with an autistic child?

Ah yes, vacation! British poet Vita Sackville-West writes, "Travel is the most private of pleasures" (Caws 2002), and Antoine de Saint-Exupéry, French novelist, swears that, "He who would travel happily must travel light." Both bring to mind peaceful sojourns, by car, plane, or even train. The mode of transportation is not what is important, what is important is *private* pleasurable travel and traveling *light*. Can't you just picture it?

It's a good bet that neither Sackville-West nor Saint-Exupéry traveled with an autistic child, and perhaps neither even traveled with a neurotypical child, because all parents know—we can't travel in private and we can't travel light!

Before Jon was diagnosed we made our first airplane trip to California. Going out was such a breeze. Jon was three years old, everything was new and exciting to him. I had read up on traveling with a preschool-age child and had a back-pack full of toys and books he had never seen before. I had also packed his chicken nuggets (which the stewardess warmed up for me), and a drink box, so he was a happy traveler.

The return trip was another story, and can be summed up as the "trip from hell," which I'm sure all of the other passengers agreed with. Jon was tired, nothing was new or exciting, and he didn't want to sit in his seat, sit on my lap, or even be in close proximity of our seats. What was I to do? I couldn't let him wander up and down the aisles, so I told him, no. NO. Several times, no. Remember toddler tantrums? (Maybe you are still experiencing them.) Remember autism + toddler tantrums = worse? Jon decided to throw one, which in his case meant lying down on the floor, face pressed into the carpet and wailing; but, unfortunately, his face pressed into the carpet didn't muffle his screams.

He proceeded to do this, lying at our feet, in the space available between the seats. Is it possible to stop a child who is having one of these tantrums?—Sometimes. Was it possible to stop my son at this point?—No. I tried to reason with him. Remember, we didn't realize this was autism and tantrums, we just thought he was extremely good at what he was doing. So, having read the experts books on toddlers who throw fits, I tried everything in the book: distraction, food, bribery (with food), a stern voice. The last thing on the list was to ignore him, and that's what my husband and I tried to do. I can still remember the looks from the other passengers as we sat with a wailing child at our feet. Yes, he was miserable; we were miserable; and everyone around us was miserable. It wasn't a pleasurable trip and it's one that I will never forget!

Of course *after* diagnosis, which in our case didn't happen until the end of kindergarten, I knew the books I should have been reading were—"How to travel with an autistic or Asperger's child." I haven't found one concise book on the subject, but I did piece together a few rules of thumb. Remember, these are Jon-specific, but they may work with your child also:

- *Food*—Pack enough not only to feed the child, but distract the child. It won't kill them to eat through a six-pack of hotdogs in a day's travel. A balanced diet?–No. But letting them eat their way through their favorite food does lead to a more peaceful trip. It used to be nuggets with Jon, now it's hotdogs and plums. (What a combination!)

- *Busy-bag—Do pack that backpack full of "new" toys, books, and games, which the experts suggest for any* child. This of course works with autistic children too, and if you pack an item that they happen to be obsessing about at the time, it works even better. Coming back from one California Christmas trip Jon insisted on carrying his new ten-pound *Ripley's Believe It or Not* book. Did I care?—No, as long as he knew he had to lug it around. And talk about a wonderful distraction! The Ripley's people surely write their books for my autistic son. Where else can he find a boat-load of strange facts, which can quickly be memorized and repeated to other people?

- *Pillows and Blankets (cuddles)*—Yes, my son is older now, but he still has his favorite pillow-cases and a blanket from his younger days. I find if I pack the pillow-cases to put on the pillows when we arrive at our destination, this makes him happy. Also, the blanket comes out on the plane and he covers his head with it when he is feeling stressed. Do I mind other people staring at my tall teenager with a blanket over his head?—Not a bit. Did you notice the man sleeping in first class with an airline blanket over his head to block out noise and light?

- *Electronics*—Yes, we are living in the computer age and quite a few of our autistic youngsters are computer whizzes. We made two airplane trips with my husband's laptop computer. Jon was in heaven—literally no less! He played solitaire to his heart's content. He played a few computer games that I let him bring with him, and I purchased *The Grinch* on DVD. Yes, post 9/11 it is more difficult to travel with a laptop computer, but the pleasure it brings my son far outweighs the long unpacking and search that we have to go through to carry it on the plane. One note about hand-held games like Game Boy, do pack extra batteries in your carry-on luggage. Nothing puts the brakes on a peaceful trip faster than battery failure!

What do we do on vacation?

This will be very child-specific, but we've found that if we plan on doing things that Jon likes to do *first*, then he will usually cooperate and do things the family wishes to do next. The first day we were in Las Vegas we found the local library so Jon could play on the internet, browse their children's section and also go through their mini-Discovery Museum. Later that week he was then persuaded to attend a live stage show of the family version of the famous Folies Bergere dancers. He actually recognized some of the show tunes during the show, and wasn't miserable the *entire* time.

Of course, when we made our trip to Disney World, Florida, it was all about Jon. But this was fine, because we had been planning for a year to be there for the "millennium." We stayed seven days, visited all four theme parks and had a really great time! Jon was even forced to see some of the "shows" he didn't want to see, and encouraged to ride some of the rides he didn't want to ride. Several years later he is still talking about it and wants to go back.

I have to add, that the minute we arrived in the first park I went to guest services and explained that my son was autistic and had trouble waiting in long lines, etc. Thereafter, guest services in every park were very helpful and filled out a "special needs" pass for us. This is the same pass they fill out for people in wheelchairs, or any other needs, and honestly, this is what saved the vacation for us. We still had to wait in lines, but they were much shorter, similar to a super-pass, as some parks called them. I explained to my son that this is what this was, a *super pass* for us.

In addition to doing what Jon wants to do first, as a trade-off for later, he and I often share downtime together. Being away from home, even staying with relatives whom we love can be very stressful for Jon. So he and I do the mall, bookstores, and even a department store once because it was the only option for us. Just this hour of wandering around in a familiar environment calmed him down and seemed to recharge him to face the relatives or the demands of the rest of the trip.

A few other important things to take on vacation:

- *Paperbacks*—for you. Because your child will have several moments of enjoyment on this trip, either in the car or on the plane, and you will want to read that latest romance/mystery/thriller/biography you have been putting off.

- *Needlework*—for you. Because if you are fortunate enough to be visiting family, they can give you some respite and watch your child for you while you try to finish that Christmas stocking you were going to do for your baby's first Christmas. Who cares that he is now in his teens, someone else will be having a baby!

- *Patience*—for you. Because if ever you will need it, it is going to be on this vacation.

  And if you are traveling with a spouse or significant other, feel free to let him or her take over the childcare for longer amounts of time. It's your vacation too, and why shouldn't you get a break from being a mom?

On one plane trip we happened to be flying on my birthday. It was four days before Christmas and the plane was packed with people and luggage. When we finally took our seats, we realized that we had not been given three seats together. At first I was upset, but then I had a brilliant idea. I would let my son sit with my husband. Jon didn't mind one way or the other and my husband laughed when he realized what I was up to. Once in the air, Jon was seated on my husband's far side, I was one row back and across the aisle from them. I immediately pulled out my book and settled down for a good uninterrupted read.

When the beverage cart came around, I ordered a glass of white wine and told the stewardess that the man one row up was buying me a drink. She quirked an eyebrow at me, but continued up the aisle and succeeded in collecting from my husband. He looked over his shoulder and I raised my glass to him. "Happy birthday to me!" I mouthed. He raised his diet cola in a toast (one of us needed to stay alert!), and he went back to watching Jon play on his game.

This was the best airplane ride I'd ever taken. I was relaxed by the time we landed, I'd had time to read my book and felt like I was ready to take on the vacation. So a word to the wise; if you are the one making the plane reservations, you may want to mention that you don't mind if they can't get all of the seats together. In doing so, you may succeed in doing what Vita Sackville-West suggests and make your travel a "private pleasure." As for Antoine de Saint-Exupéry's suggestion on traveling light? One out of two isn't bad!

When can we, or our son, *start traveling alone?*

chicken nugget #6

On perseveration—"Stop beating that dead horse!"

> Against boredom even the gods themselves struggle in vain.
>
> *(Nietzsche)*

What in the world is perseveration, and what do we do about it? *The Oxford English Dictionary* defines this term as "repeating or prolonging an action, thought or utterance after the stimulus that prompted it has ceased." We as parents might define this as: "My child latches on to a thing, topic or interest and literally beats it to death. He or she won't shut up about it, doesn't lose interest in it, and basically just drives me nuts about it!"

Both definitions are valid in my book. In addition, in Bryna Siegel's book *The World of the Autistic Child*, she discusses "the perseveration of sensory play." Here she describes the perseveration of a younger child who is so fascinated with a pull toy that makes a noise, and who pulls this toy not five or six times but for twenty minutes or more. She explains that this perseveration is not unique to autism, but what is unique is "for the autistic child, being interrupted while engaged in a favorite perseverative activity can be like having someone switch off the TV at the most suspenseful part of a movie" (Siegel 1996, p.63). They get more upset than a neurotypical child would at this point. At the same time she discusses "preoccupying, narrow interests of the persons with Asperger's Syndrome" (p.115) or high-functioning autism, and the fact that when talking to this individual, it doesn't take long for this special topic of interest to come up. Not only does it come up, but trying to get this individual off of this topic is like trying to get a dog away from a bone, or, trying to get them to stop beating that dead horse (my analogy, not Siegel's!).

We first noticed this when Jon was old enough to watch videos and began talking. This was also about the same time that he was diagnosed in kindergarten. His topic of interest was Dr. Seuss; the books, the videos, it didn't matter. Everything was Seuss. He would tell everyone a Dr. Seuss story that he had just watched or read. But he wouldn't just tell them about it, he would repeat it, word for word, from beginning to end. We of course noticed immediately his amazing ability to memorize and were fascinated. It wouldn't be long before his topic of interest would change and he told us *Gargoyle* stories after watching the series on TV. Next came Garfield comic books, where he not only repeated the comic strips from page to page, cover to cover, but would act them out too. After this it was any Disney movie that was currently playing.

Yes, it was fascinating, and amazing, but believe me when I say, it gets to be old after you have heard his current topic of "conversation" more than five times. Many times we explained, "Okay, you told me that already and I don't need to hear it again." When he was little and into children's game shows we began imitating the game-show buzzer.

" ...and then Garfield says to Odie..."

"Bzzzzz...time's up! New topic!" It worked for a while.

Siegel adds: "It is quite possible and not harmful to them, to impose limits on repetitious talk" (p.116). She explains that in doing so, you help to teach them correct conversation skills, and if you take their compulsive interest of the moment it is possible to turn it into a more appropriate discussion. For example, with Jon and Garfield we could have said, "Do you think you can draw that comic or write your own comic?" (This might have led us to finding out earlier that he had an interest in drawing cartoons.) After all, our goal is to teach him more normal behaviors and this would have been an opportune moment.

Does this mean I do not let my child persevervate at all on his current topic of interest?—This is a more difficult question to answer. My son is autistic. No matter how high-functioning he is, it is always there. He will always want to perseverate about something—it comes with the territory. How do I help him, while allowing him also to be just who he is?

We have discovered one way of dealing with this. There was a TV show called *Mister Rogers' Neighbourhood*, in which Fred Rogers sang a song that went something like "Let's think of something to do while we're waiting...while we're waiting—something to do." Jon watched Mr. Rogers, and for some reason, this song has stayed with me. I began to wonder, what if we allowed Jon to perseverate on his topic only when other (neurotypical) children would also be experiencing boredom and looking for "something to do." It is very normal behavior to be waiting, or driving long-distance in the car, and play silly word games, sing songs, or tell riddles and jokes. Why couldn't we just let Jon have it?

What a breakthrough this was for us. Soon after deciding on this tactic we had to drive to an airport about four hours away. We let Jon sing all of his *Veggie Tale* songs to us. On the plane ride, he was allowed to tell one of us "a story" as long as he interspersed it with reading the book he had brought with him and giving the listener a break once in a while. When we were at Disneyland, standing in line for a ride, we would also let him tell us whatever he wished during the wait time. And later, dealing with an hour flight delay, my husband and I took turns listening to a verbal recitation of one of his favorite videos.

It worked! Jon was happy, we were not being driven too crazy, and he was only perseverating during times when everyone else would also be bored and looking for a distraction.

Several years later, as Jon entered High School, this strategy still works, and we've added to it. To help Jon to become more aware of what is going on around him, *in the moment*, we are trying to teach him to look first before launching into one of his "stories." For example, when I'm driving he has learned that I can't listen to him and negotiate traffic at the same time. He now looks to see how the traffic flow is before continuing. (This lesson learned after a few near accidents!) And Dad is working on teaching him to try to pay attention to the person he is talking to, to see if that person is bored with the topic or really interested. This still needs a little work because Jon stops talking mid-sentence and asks, "Am I boring you?" How many folks out there besides his parents are going to honestly tell him yes?

Jon continues to work with his speech teacher on learning scripted conversations, and how and when to change topic. He's also learning how to actually listen when the other person is talking instead of zoning out until it's his turn to talk.

Pretty basic stuff for a youth in High School. But I have it from the best authority (see interview with a school counselor, Chapter 9), that all students at this age need help with social skills. Jon's help is just a little more specific, in that he has to learn actual conversation skills by rote.

Yes, we've learned what perseveration is. We deal with it daily. But like anything in life, we had to find our own happy medium. We had to learn the best way to deal with this integral part of our son, not only understanding it, but working *with* it so that we can keep from constantly telling him, "All right, that's enough!"

Alas, I do admit that at times, when he is going on and on and on, that I'm not really paying attention. I'm nodding "a huh" and saying "oh yeah?" But there is a song playing in my head that goes "Let's think of something to do while we're waiting…while we're waiting—something to do."

Why can't I get him to perseverate on his algebra, history, or science?

Chapter Seven

What about anger?

Just because your child has a disability, doesn't make you a doormat!

> I have a right to my anger, and I don't want anybody telling me I shouldn't be, that it's not nice to be, and that something's wrong with me because I get angry.
>
> *(Maxine Waters, California congresswoman)*

Will it hurt my child if I get angry at him or her?

I yelled at my son today. Yes, my autistic son, there is no other. I am making him take tennis lessons. Making, as in—he hates it. He has tried and stopped several other sports and would happily sit in front of his computer or his TV every minute of every day. But this time, I've put my foot down. He will take tennis lessons this summer or I will die trying to make him. Hmm…do I really want to declare that? A possible premonition of my early demise?

Nevertheless, he did the first three-week session, meeting twice a week and actually learned to connect the racket with the ball and hit it over the net (the ball, not the racket!). And today, he began his next three-week session. This class is larger, five girls and four boys. They actually will be hitting the ball, at each other, later on. So today I sat and watched with a little more trepidation.

He did pretty well. They played the regular bounce-the-ball-games and then got in some good practice with hitting it over the net. He still had major difficulty with an overhand serve, but he didn't lose his cool (although he was dripping with sweat, his least favorite thing).

Then they came to one last game. They were to run the baselines, boys against the girls, and I'm sure this was to teach them good foot work, sliding backwards, and so on. Jon was the last in the line. He always puts himself last when lining up for things. The boys were winning until it was his turn. He started out great. Everyone was yelling encouragement. Then came his autistic moment. He quit in the middle of the race. He walked the rest of the baselines. Boy, were his team-mates mad! They continued to yell at him to "move it!" He finished behind the girl, and slammed his racket onto the net in frustration. I had sat without a word to him the entire hour, but now I angrily yelled his name across the court. He looked up as if he had forgotten that I was there and shouted, "Sorry! Sorry!"

The class ended. The teacher told him he had done a good job. He *had* been the winner in the ball balancing game. I made him drink his water on the way to the car and held back my comments. Then when we got to the car I let him have it. I didn't raise my voice, that would have caused an instant shutdown, but I gave him both barrels of my anger.

I told him he had done great the entire hour until the last game. He had lost any rewards he had earned just by quitting during that game and then reacting angrily by slamming his racket when he lost. I told him he was a teenager, not three years old, and that games and competition were a part of life and growing up. Tennis was just a game. He needed to learn to compete and not be a quitter. I told him he had tried baseball and quit. Basketball, quit. Soccer, quit. Taekwondo, quit. I would not let him sit on his rear-end the rest of the summer and be a couch potato. He was going to learn some tennis and get some exercise and he just better get used to it!

He began sniffling. I began instantly to feel guilty.

I then apologized for yelling at him while he was on the court, but I also told him that he was very smart and could do this if he would just not be a quitter. I told him that I yelled at him because I loved him and I knew he could do this. I added that I just didn't know how to make him get this into his head.

He cried and sniffled and put up his hand and said, "Wait, I'm trying to say something." I waited. He told me he had gotten it. He wanted to do sports. He didn't want to be a couch potato. "You've knocked some sense into me," he said.

After his shower, he came to me and asked, "When can I go walk around the block with you? (I'm trying to lose weight and have a two-mile course set out.) I tell him, "Later, when it's cooler," and we shake on it.

Wow. What has happened here? I wonder. Will this last? Maybe it will this time. I can only be positive and hope for the best.

I did learn one main principle here. Yes, my son is autistic, but he isn't a fragile piece of glass. All children need to hear a stern voice once in a while. Sometimes it takes a stern voice to get through to them. I'm not talking "screemie-meemie" here, I'm talking controlled anger, so that my child knew that I was serious and very upset with him.

I remember reading somewhere about a dad with an autistic child. The child would have rages and become destructive. One day this child actually became so angry that they threw something through the TV screen. The dad totally freaked out and yelled at the child, "This cannot continue! This absolutely cannot happen again!" Then he wrote that the most amazing thing happened. The child listened, heard him, and the rages got better. Life didn't suddenly become perfect, but better.

I read that story a long time ago, when my son was very little. I don't use that story to justify my anger towards my son, but to remind myself other parents are human like I am. And now, when I yell at him about tennis and sports and being a couch potato, I suddenly wonder if we too have had a breakthrough just as that man and his child did?

I won't know of course until the next thing comes along that he wants to participate in, but this I know for sure, just because my son is autistic, doesn't mean I have to be a doormat!

Do parents of neurotypical children worry about yelling too much at their kids, or is this mostly an us issue?

chicken nugget #7

"I love you, but we are not connected at the hip!"

God could not be everywhere, so he made mothers.

(Jewish proverb)

When does mother-love become smother-love?

When I wrote a chapter on the history of autism for my first book, *Parent to Parent: Information and Inspiration for Parents Dealing with Autism or Asperger's Syndrome*, I read with interest about the first theories of autism. Kanner was supposed to have coined the phrase "refrigerator mom" but I found out it was the US *Time* magazine reporter who put the fatal words in Kanner's mouth. And poor Kanner, he was probably asked about this until his dying day. His original theory was that the autistic children he was studying seemed all to come from highly successful, busy parents. Because of this similarity in family occupations and IQ levels of the parents, he postulated that perhaps these children were autistic because they were lacking some degree of maternal love from birth because the mother was a working, busy mom. The reporter jumped in and said: "like a cold or refrigerator mother" and the phrase was born. Kanner, from that interview on, was constantly challenged on this and eventually did say he was misquoted and an erroneous conclusion had been made.

Of course any mother of an autistic child could tell the experts that this is ridiculous. It has now been shown that working mothers, at 60 million now in the US, may be too loving to their children. The reason may be that working moms surely feel more guilt in raising their children because they can't be home with them, and as a result, try to make up for this by being overprotective, overloving, and develop what some call *smother-love*.

When Jon was diagnosed in kindergarten we went through the normal grief cycle that most parents do when they are told their beautiful child has a disability. The only difference I could see between myself and perhaps other parents who went through this same cycle, was that I went through at warp speed. After his diagnosis on May 31, I rapidly went through all of the stages in about 30 days: anger, denial, right on through to acceptance, so that I called the school on July 1 and told the Special Services Director, "Okay, you are right, now what do I do?" Later she told me she didn't know who I was until several minutes into the conversation, since she wasn't expecting to hear from us for some time.

From that moment on, I continued at warp speed. I learned, as I've said, that knowledge brought peace of mind. So I read, researched, and attended conferences in search of that peace. Thank goodness, I did find peace, but did I stop there?—No.

Now that I had all of this knowledge, I quickly realized there was no one else on this earth who loved Jon enough to become his advocate. So I worked at becoming that too.

But advocating meant a little more in my mind than just helping Jon out. To me, as an advocate for my son, I not only try to help him, I support, defend, and often plead his case for him. I read to become the expert in *his* expression of autism, and I read to learn how I should express myself on his behalf. Of course it's a time-consuming job. What advocate's job (read *parent's* here) isn't?

However, a few years back I suddenly began to wonder about this connection I had with my son. He had attended a local summer camp for one week, two summers in a row, and this particular summer, he refused to go.

His reason? "I'll miss you."

Okay. This was typical kid behavior, but this behavior was supposed to go away as the typical child grew older. It seemed that Jon, who had only been slightly clingy as a younger child was now into full-blown cling, at the age of 12. My husband and I discussed this, and tried to come up with answers. Our family support base had grown smaller as my husband's family moved West, so there was really no one watching Jon for us so we could take a break, even for an evening. Thus, we began to make a special effort to find places for Jon to go visit without us—my sister's house a couple of hours north, a school friend's house just for a late evening (Jon still refuses to spend the night over at this friend's).

It was at this time when I first told Jon, "I love you, but we are not connected at the hip!" I demonstrated this physically, by putting my hip next to his, and moving away from him.

That summer, I planned a weekend getaway with my sister, just the girls, getting away to shop. Jon wanted so badly to go. He did not want to stay home with Dad. I told him, no, this was just a mom thing, and "I love you, but we are not connected at the hip."

A few months later, I attended a short autism conference about four hours away. Jon knew this city had a zoo, and a wonderful mall for shopping, but once again I told him he could not go with me. Not only was it a conference for parents and professionals, but I wanted to attend without having to worry about what to do with him while I was in the sessions.

School started, Jon had another birthday, and slowly got used to staying home by himself, for an hour or so in the evenings, if my husband and I wanted to go out. We quickly learned that if he had shows that he wanted to watch on TV, such as *Cartoon-Cartoon-Fridays*, he would be fine being home alone. But once his shows were over, he would start calling us to see when we were coming home. Usually we tried to time things so that by the time he made the second call, we were done with our dinner or movie and were on our way.

The next summer I went on another road trip with my sister, this time for about four days instead of a weekend. But I didn't have to give Jon *the phrase* when he asked if he could go. I started to tell him, "No, because…" and Jon jumped in and said, "Because we are not joined at the hip!" I was elated, he seemed to be getting it.

Getting it so well that recently, for the first time in my son's life, I went out of town, by myself, for seven days. My husband had been gone 11 days to his family's home out West, so I told myself I surely deserved this week alone.

As the date drew closer, and Jon and I talked about me going, he would say, "Ah…I'm going to miss you…" I would reply, "Yes, but you and Dad will have a good time for a week. And you can call me on my cell phone." My husband and I had agreed that if this was going to work, I had to be reachable by phone, at any time.

The day arrived, and I left to drive to my conference on a Sunday morning at 6:00 a.m. Once there I found that because I was staying on a college campus, not only did I not have a phone in my room, but no TV either. I soon realized how alone I was when I called home the first night to tell Jon good-night. He and Dad had just been to the Ripley's Museum (from the creators of *Ripley's Believe It or Not*), and he was very excited about it. "I can't wait for you to come home so you can go too," he said. We said our good-nights and I told him I would talk to him the next day.

This became the daily routine. I would turn the phone on vibrate while in class, since Jon had quickly memorized the phone number, and was allowed to call me whenever he wanted to. He and I would speak twice a day, maybe more, and I would call late at night to tell them good-night. He and Dad tried to do something special every night, whether go to a show or go over to his cousins for a barbecue, and as the week progressed I couldn't believe how much I missed my son. He was doing fine. I was going through withdrawal!

Not only did I not have a TV to distract me, but over half of my life was missing for seven days—my son, my husband, and the cat. For one solid week I wasn't my son's advocate, I was just a mom calling home. It was a very eye-opening experience, and I began to wonder who was dependent on whom? Had raising my son, advocating for his disability, become so all-consuming that *I* was the one who was still connected at the hip. And if so, what could I do about this?

Recently I was able to leave the office early on Saturday. Jon was home playing on his video games and watching Saturday shows. (No Playstation or TV during the school week in our house. This is the only way we can keep Jon focused on school.) I called him to say I was coming home early and was going to go to the bookstore. This particular store has a cat as the *owner* and Jon has always enjoyed not only going and digging through the used books, but also tracking down Calvin-the-cat.

Imagine my surprise when he said, "No, I don't want to go. I'm fine here."

I quickly made a left turn instead of a right towards the house and said, "Are you sure? You haven't seen Calvin in a while."

"Na, I'm fine, and they don't really have any books I like."

I slowly headed towards the bookstore. Hmm… I could almost hear in my head Jon saying, "Mom, we are not connected at the hip!" Of course I had been trying to get him to realize this for the past several years, but when it finally happened and I realized that my teenage son didn't want to hang out with me any more, it made me stop and think *mom* thoughts: my baby is growing up; he doesn't necessarily want to be with Mom any more, and, well…I asked for it, didn't I?

I found a very interesting, and slightly upsetting, quote by writer Dorothy L. Sayers: "Those who make some other person their job are dangerous." Oh my! Does this apply to me? Have I become dangerous to my son, and myself? Well...hopefully, not yet.

Because now I know—I know that I can love my son and learn not to smother him. I know that as I continue to advocate, support, and stick up for my son, I can also begin to create a little distance between us. And already, with the beginning of High School, the opportunity has arrived.

In trying to teach Jon more independence, we are making him fill in his daily homework planner, and take all questions to his teachers. He still has an aide for the moment, but she is only checking his planner and helping him learn to become more independent.

The second week of school, as we pulled out of the parking lot at the end of the day, I asked Jon if he had asked his caseworker when he could volunteer in the school library. He had written the question down in his notebook that morning and was supposed to come up with the answer.

He literally scratched his head and said, "Oh...I asked her."

"And?"

"And... I don't remember what she said."

"Why is that?"

"Well...she answered, but I don't remember."

I could very well picture Jon asking the question, and then zoning out during the answer. He of course still has problems with social skills, conversational listening, and so on.

Then he said, "I think you should come in and talk to Mrs. Wright. You're a good negotiator!"

Did I make a left turn back into the parking lot instead of a right turn towards home? Not this time. I smiled and kept driving.

"No. You are a good negotiator too. You just need to pay particular attention when you ask a question and try to hear the answer."

He wrote the question down in his notebook to ask it again the following day and in the distance I thought I heard a tearing noise. Purse strings? Apron strings? Cloth from us being connected at the hip? It will get easier for me. But what's hard is realizing that I'm soon to be out of a job!

How independent can my high-functioning autistic son learn to become?

Chapter Eight

Straight talk for parents

"We need to be like the Energizer Bunny, we must keep going and going…"

Should I demand things for my child that others may not like?

Leo Buscaglia writes in his book, *The Disabled and Their Parents*, "Families of the disabled have rights, too. Everyone would benefit greatly if each family member and each professional involved would honor and respect these rights" (1983, p.109). This book came out long before my child was even born, but after Jon's diagnosis I began searching for a copy of it. Not because there weren't any other books out there to read, but because I had read Buscaglia's other books, such as *Living, Loving and Learning* (1982), and I felt that since he knew so much about relationships and life, surely he would also understand what I was going through.

I found a used copy and quickly read it from cover to cover, learning that I had been right. Buscaglia knew what he was talking about. In a nutshell, what Buscaglia says is that parents and families of the disabled do have rights, and it is our duty not only to fight for the rights of our disabled children, but our families' rights as well.

After reading this book, I almost felt sorry for the special services staff at the school Jon was attending. For when we showed up at the end of the year IEP meeting to get ready for second grade, suddenly they were dealing with a different me! Gone was the parent who had sat and cried the year before while reading the first 14-page IEP that was handed to her, and in her place was a future parent from hell.

This time, when they handed me the written IEP, I took out a pen and began writing on it. I also pulled out a stack of papers, questions, thoughts, and suggestions that I had brought with me, passed copies around to the other team members and said, "Okay, now I'm ready to write next year's IEP."

You see, after learning from Buscaglia that I had rights, I began reading about those rights, and I learned that IEPs are supposed to be written as a *group* effort, most importantly with the parent or guardian's input. I also learned that there were a lot of things I could ask for pertaining to my child's education, from environment in the classroom, to how the lessons are taught or re-taught for him. My husband's motto has always been "It doesn't hurt to ask," and we immediately applied this to our son's IEP.

When it became stressful for Jon to attend the all-school assemblies because of the noise level in the gym, we asked that he first be given the choice not to attend, and second, if he did wish to attend, it would be agreed that if during the assembly he became too agitated, he would be allowed to leave. We also purchased headphones for him to wear, the type that people use on shooting ranges, and this helped him sit through the assemblies. Eventually he graduated to not needing the headphones, but he is still allowed to leave if the noise level or "rowdiness" is too high.

Later, we asked that he be given extra time to finish assignments, if this is what was needed. Usually this meant he could stay in during a recess or later in the day, and move into the special services room to finish a test or an assignment. This still applies and is one thing that has allowed him to stay up with his peers in all academic subjects, resulting in mostly A and B work.

Because of Buscaglia's book I was able to speak quite frankly when we were moving into a new school district at the beginning of third grade. This school was three times the size of the one we were coming from, and I told the Special Services Director and her caseworker, I was not the type of parent to sit and let things just move along. I was my son's advocate and in moving to a bigger school district I would not allow my son just to become a number or a case file. My husband later told me that while I was looking down at the notes I had brought with me, both of their mouths were open in slight surprise. "Good!" I told him.

Soon after moving into this new school district, I also became a card-carrying member of a group called the MFH (Mothers From Hell 2). This group sends out a quarterly bulletin of stories and jokes, anecdotes and even sometimes serious issues about how we as the MFH can advocate for our children. They can still be found at their website at www.mothersfromhell2.org.

Recently a situation came up where, once again, I had to put my foot down. My son began a short summer school program on basic computer software. He had the choice of taking this class over the course of a normal three-month semester in High School, or taking the same class for three weeks during the summer before. When I explained this to him, even my son, who has to learn common sense issues, saw the obvious sense in taking the class in the summer.

He started one week after school was over and we soon fell into a routine. I would drop him off at the doors of his future High School, he would disappear inside, and five hours later I would be waiting to pick him up. One day I was early or the class was late, and my son was a long time coming out the front doors. I got out of the car and strolled over to where other kids were milling about waiting for their rides.

When Jon come out, I watched his face light up as he saw me and then just as quickly he flinched and covered the side of his face with his hand. As I took all this in, I saw the kids he had just walked by break out into laughter. When he got in the car I asked, "Did someone say something to you as you were coming out the door?" The year before in Junior High we had dealt with a very serious bully situation that had turned into daily harassment in school.

"No," Jon said.

Okay, I thought, and rephrased the question. "Did someone sing something at you?" I had learned to be very specific in my questions.

"Yeah," he muttered. "You know, the usual song that they know I don't like."

Immediately I was outraged. I thought this had all stopped at the Junior High the year before. Several of the kids had learned how to push Jon's buttons so that at one point every hall he walked down there was a kid there taunting him or singing at him.

I went back to work and told my husband about what had happened. I also told him that I was not going to put up with any more of this! I felt I had waited too long the year before, possibly allowing the situation to grow worse, and I wasn't going to do that again. My husband agreed that I should do what I felt I had to do but warned me not to "burn any bridges" at the High School since Jon had to attend there next year.

I mulled this over in my mind and didn't sleep good, but the next morning I was ready.

Instead of dropping Jon off at the doors, I parked the car.

"Where are you going?" he asked.

"I want to meet your teacher and your aide," I said. After all, it was only day four of the summer class.

He was okay with this, and I followed him inside.

As he went to get his teacher, I saw the aide approaching, took a few deep breaths, and hoped for the right words. The last time I had talked to a teacher about bullying I had not been able to stay calm.

His teacher and aide were soon standing with me in the hall. I explained to them that not only was I simply wanting to meet them face to face, but that a possible problem had arisen with another student. I gave them his name, and described who he was, just in case Jon had perhaps gotten the wrong name. I told them what Jon had said, that this was one of the boys who had picked on Jon almost the entire year before. I explained that we had gotten it stopped during the last few months of the school year, but imagine my dismay to learn that on only the third day of computer class here we were again. Both teachers were very surprised and very supportive.

I took a deep breath and said, "You know, I feel it was my fault about last year going on so long, but sometimes I walk a fine line between being an advocate for my son and being a parent from hell. Last year I may have been afraid to cross that line. But right now, I don't care if you think I am a mother from hell, I will *not* allow my son to be harassed by this boy every day of summer school!"

Ah! I learned first hand what a pregnant pause really was. Both teachers were speechless for a moment. I stopped talking and let my words hang in the air.

After a long moment, the computer teacher placed her hand on my arm. "I understand perfectly, and we will not let this boy do this to Jon any more. I am so glad you came in and spoke to us."

I thanked them both, told my son, who had just approached us, to have a good day in computer class, and left. Getting to the car, I immediately called my husband on my cell phone and told him about the conversation.

"What was their response?" he asked.

"All positive," I said.

"Well, we will see what happens," came his somewhat pessimistic reply.

We waited. I quizzed Jon daily, rephrasing the key questions, and to our delight, there was never another instance during the entire three weeks of class where someone taunted him or sang at him. I don't know what the teacher or aide did, but they did take care of the problem.

What did I learn from this? That I didn't have to step over the line and become a screaming mom to get help. I was able to be honest with his teachers and they responded in kind. Or maybe it was the threat that I could be a mother from hell that motivated them to deal with the situation? My husband thinks it is the latter! But it doesn't matter to me. We got the response we needed!

When advocating for my child, and sometimes it is we vs. they in our IEP meetings, does it ever bother me that others may perceive me as a parent from hell? Honestly?—Yes and No.

Yes, because it is natural for anyone, including myself, to want to be liked. No, because when it comes right down to it, if I don't put my foot down and sometimes be that parent from hell for Jon, who will? No one else will go to bat for him in the bottom of the ninth with the bases loaded like I will. And if it comes right down to either taking a charge from someone like basketball great Shaquille O'Neal, or losing it all? I am there, ready to get plowed into. Seriously, putting sport metaphors aside, when I get hurt, I get over it. I'm an adult. God knows I've been through worse things than having someone think bad things about me, or say bad things about me. But when my son gets hurt emotionally or, heaven forbid, physically, it may take a long time for him to get over it.

This is why we must be like that famous bunny. It doesn't matter what others may think or say, we can be the parents from hell and we keep going and going and… (you get the picture) for the rest of our son's life. Leo Buscaglia taught me long ago that this was my right as a parent of a disabled child, and I continue to take him at his word.

If I am the best advocate for my child, who will do this if something happens to me?

Birthday parties—so simple, yet so impossible

There is still no cure for the common birthday.

(John Glenn, astronaut and senator)

Will my son ever enjoy normal things like birthday parties?

I believe there is a room in heaven called the "Birthday Room." In this room there is a continuing birthday party in our honor. We enter the room and the party starts. We don't have to lift a finger—everything is ready. The food, cake, decorations, and entertainment are set up, functioning, and we didn't have to put them there or plan it. We get to stay in this room as long as we wish. The guests have already arrived and they are only people we wish to party with. We can leave at any time and don't have to pick up a plate, or cup, unless it is to eat out of, or drink out of. We can return to this room again and again, and it will always be the perfect birthday party in our honor.

Why a "Birthday Room"? Because all of us moms, and dads, who plan all of the birthday parties during our child's lifetime, need some type of reward! I agree with John Glenn. There is still no cure for the birthday and, I add, for the birthday party. Glenn was probably bemoaning the age issue, I'm bemoaning the party itself. Parents with neurotypical children have a difficult time planning and pulling off a successful birthday party, how much more difficult it is with our autistic children!

I don't know about your child, but we discovered at an early age, Jon doesn't like birthday parties. The same year when he was beginning to be tested to see if there was something wrong, we planned a birthday party at "Chuckie Cheese"—the loud, crazy-fun pizza hall. We met at the location, a few friends, their kids and close family members, opened the hallowed front door and lined up to begin our party. Jon went wild, kicking, screaming, and crying. Looking back, I realize it was the instant noise level that set him off: zinging machines, musical dancing animals, and kids shrieking, having a wonderful time. It was way too much for him and we couldn't get him through those front doors.

I looked at my husband, shook my head and, turning to the small group of family and friends, said, "Let's meet at the McDonalds up the street." McDonalds! Music to my son's ears. He calmed down immediately and we piled back into our cars and drove off. Once there, we fed the kids those wonderful kids' meals that make them happy, and sat and watched them play on the playground, which, because it was October, we had all to ourselves. The staff quickly thawed out a birthday cake for us and the birthday party was saved!

As Jon grew up, we realized that it wasn't just noise level that caused him not to like birthdays, he didn't like the birthday party itself. It was the following year that he ran screaming from the room when everyone sang Happy Birthday to him. Unfortunately, this happened at school with well-meaning classmates, and soon we realized that although he still wanted to have birthday parties, he didn't enjoy them once they were in full swing.

What a quandary this became. Do we have a party or not? (Without the birthday song of course.)

As the years passed, we usually opted out of having the party. We would have a small gathering with family only, no singing allowed, and he seemed satisfied with this. But at the beginning of seventh grade he suddenly wanted to plan a party, invitations and all, and to have it at the local pizza place (not the noisy one). I agreed. We made invitations on the computer; Jon invited his one friend from school, a few teachers he liked, his aide and his principal. Family members were a given.

We arrived at the party room to find minimal decorations, which I had suggested, and the guests soon began to arrive. After Jon realized that one teacher and the principal were not coming (thank goodness his aide showed up!), he began to shut down.

No. He didn't want to open his presents. He didn't want to participate. He was bummed that the other two hadn't shown up.

What did I do?—I *forced* him to have a good time (yeah, right!). What else could I do? I explained to him that not everyone could come all of the time, and that he needed to enjoy those guests who were here. I *forced* him to open his presents and say thank you, even if he didn't like the present, and I *forced* him to eat pizza with the rest of us. The no-singing had long been implemented, so there was no problem there. But we do have pictures of this birthday. Everyone is smiling, Jon is pouting. Oh, what fun!

When we arrived at his fourteenth year, Jon wanted to invite some friends from school to have a party at the house. Oh, no! I thought. Do I go there again?

Yes, I do. What's a mother to do?

We made the invitations on the computer; we invited his best friend, a girl he liked at school, and another girl who was nice to him in Spanish class. As the day grew closer, one girl couldn't come. Then the girl that he liked couldn't come. Every day when I picked him up at school I could tell who was coming by the look on his face. Several days before the event I explained to him that people do have other things going on in their life and maybe we should invite family and cousins.

"No," he said. "I'm not ever inviting anyone ever again!"

I told him this was overreacting, and the party would be fine.

Two days before the party, one girl's mother called and explained that she would be coming, they had gotten an appointment wrong. Jon was once again ecstatic. We could now "un-invite" the family. (It's a good thing my family knows him well!)

The evening arrived, two girls, my son, and his buddy. We had popcorn chicken, french-fries and brownies. He had opened his presents before everyone arrived because he didn't want to do it in front of anyone. My husband came home early to support me, and we had our first "teenage" party. They watched one of his new DVDs, *Ghostbusters*, and Jon got up and went to his room a couple of times to play on his computer. His buddy joined him a few times. Then we all gathered back in the living room for the end of the movie.

The parents came and picked up their teenagers and Jon came out of his room to tell them goodbye, thanks for coming, etc.... When they left he said, "Whew, that was a little much!"

I patted him on the back and told him he had done well. I was very proud of him for "putting up with" this birthday party and having these kids in his home for a few hours. This was one party we could chalk up as a success. Maybe next year he won't have to go to his room to be by himself.

Oh, no...next year?

Maybe by then I can teach him this thought from an unknown source—"A birthday is just the first day of another 365-day journey around the sun. Enjoy the trip"—and we could forgo the party? If not, that's okay too.

I know there will be my "Birthday Room" waiting for me in heaven, and I won't have to lift a finger when I'm there!

Other cultures celebrate bithdays differently. Do we have to go with what's normal in this culture for our children? Why not create a new normal?

Chapter Nine

An interview with the school counselor

When I was a boy of fourteen, my father was so ignorant I could hardly stand to have the old man around. But when I got to be twenty-one, I was astonished by how much he'd learned in seven years.

(Mark Twain)

With my son, what is typical Junior High School behavior?

Jon is our only child, so at times it is hard for his dad and me to distinguish between what is normal kid behavior, in this case budding teenager, and what is autism. As usual, I wanted to speak to an expert for advice, and in this case it turned out to be the Junior High counselor. I'll call her Nancy.

Nancy has been a counselor for 18 years and is on the verge of retirement. I hadn't met her before, or had much interaction with her during seventh grade, because Jon had so many other IEP team members and she was not usually working with him. I called her about three months into eighth grade as adolescent vs. autism questions began entering my mind. She graciously said I could interview her and gave permission for me to use the information in this chapter. The following is our conversation.

Me: Since Jon is an only child who happens to be autistic and also a teenager, we are having trouble distinguishing between what is typical teen behavior and what is autism. Could you explain to me what is typical Junior High School behavior? What is the first thing that comes to your mind when a parent of a seventh grader asks, "What can I expect from my child over these next two Junior High years?"

Nancy: Lots of changes during these years. Hormonal changes in the body, a lot of immaturity in social skills, the desire to become more independent—they are trying to find their own identity. Therefore they are wanting to take on responsibility and be an independent person, but they are still not an adult. They still need structure from the parent, they still need those boundaries although they don't think they do. They still need that security. So this is a really tough time in their life, for both the child and the parent, simply because they are no longer a child and not an adult. However, this period is where parents have to start giving up some control of their child's life, and have to start giving up some things—but not totally.

Me: I remember my seventh and eighth grade being the worst part of my growing-up years. And I was supposedly a neurotypical child. I can't imagine any child with differences going through Junior High.

Nancy: Basically, the autistic kids are lacking in so many social skills anyway, that when they hit this age, it just compounds that problem, I think.

Me: If we are going to see different attitudes with Junior High students, I know attitude is a big thing, what is their attitude going to be toward power, authority, teachers, adults, and their own parents? Does this change during these years?

Nancy: It definitely changes toward parents. You will see some kids who rebel a little more against authority at the Junior High age. Particularly those who are not necessarily as motivated toward school. But I think all kids have a rebellious period toward parents and this goes back to them trying to gain some independence and parents having a hard time giving that up.

Me: Does their attitude change toward peers also? Toward friendships?

Nancy: Yes!

Me: How does that change? What do you see that is different?

Nancy: Peers become the most important part of their lives. More important than their parents and teachers—more than anyone. The reason is a need for acceptance, that hierarchy of need; to be accepted into a group and by their peers becomes so predominant during these years of adolescence when they are making a transition.

Me: What happens if they don't find a group by the end of eighth grade? How does this affect them? I mean, everyone seems to want to find a clique.

Nancy: I think it's very hard on them. I have more kids now who have developed depression, or anxiety disorder at this age. When I visit with them, a lot of times one of the major issues is *I have no friends at school, I don't have anyone to talk to, I don't have a best friend.* I think this becomes so important in their lives that it escalates. We may not see this as an adult, and we can look at this and tell them they have so many other things in life that they are good at—look, you are excelling in this, excelling in that. But they don't see it in the light we see it in. They see it as "I have no friends, I'm a nobody, nobody likes me, I'm unimportant," and life just becomes a worry for them instead of something which should be happy.

Me: It becomes almost escalated in their own mind because peers are so important?

Nancy: It does actually escalate and become a major problem with them.

Me: They come in from sixth grade, they are all hyped up for Junior High. Does their attitude change towards grades and homework and studying? Or are they still hyped up, wanting to perform academically?

Nancy: I'm not so sure this changes that much in Junior High. If they are motivated in the lower grades to excel and do well, they are going to come over here and want to do well. Now sometimes because of organizational skills which have not matured completely at this age, taking on the seven different classes with seven different teachers handing out homework assignments, this can become a struggle. Not necessarily not wanting to do it or not understanding it, but just being able to get organized enough to get all of the work done for each class.

Me: So, this is even typical? This is not just autistic?

Nancy: No, not at all. This is typical behavior for all the kids. And we try to help them in that area by developing the national binder system; we have the homework hotline, we give them another set of books for home. Because we know this is a time of disorganization for all students we try to help handle that.

Me: Do their interests change? I know we talked about peers but what about activities? Do interests change in seventh and eighth grade or are they still the same child as fifth and sixth grade according to their interests?

Nancy: I think their interests do change, but I think there are some interests that are lifelong. I'm talking about kids who may be involved in dance or gymnastics, or theatrical work. Those interests are just going to become stronger. I think that kids who have a strong background in religion are going to stay with that and keep with those groups at this age. Now in High School, this may change a little bit. But most of the kids try to keep their standards.

Me: If you are in the hallway and you hear conversations, what is the typical theme of conversation which you would not have heard if these were sixth graders? What is the difference in conversation and peer interaction here?

Nancy: I hear a lot about confrontations and rumors, that sort of thing going on with kids. Because their social skills are immature it's "Did you hear about such and such?" and, like any rumor, when it gets going it becomes larger and larger, bigger, and then it usually gets back to that person, and then I have that person in my office in tears and we have to try to find out what is going on. We deal a lot with social issues and relationships.

Me: Sorta like a little *Peyton Place?* Focusing on the fact that this is their little world. And you are here to help direct their little world so that they can learn to be more mature in that world.

Nancy: Yes! That's basically it. And there are so many things in that world. We have to teach them the academics, that is the primary goal here, but many times there are so many issues going on in their own personal lives that academics are way down there. They are trying to meet some of these basic needs up here, and hopefully I help them a little bit with that.

Me: We already talked about socially, what about when you said that there are maturity levels that haven't developed yet. What about boy and girl relationships, the S-word? Does this become a big issue in seventh and eighth grade? Is it all of a sudden they hit seventh grade and it's boy–girl?

Nancy: Yes! When you look at our handbook we address boy–girl relationships and it probably is not addressed until seventh grade. We say that the only contact that they can have at Junior High is holding hands. And we have to tell our seventh graders that, PDA [public display of affection] has to be dealt with.

Me: Do you see crushes? Or do you see more?

Nancy: Both. And a lot of that is that they are all developing at different stages. Some aren't interested in that relationship yet. Generally it happens that during the seventh grade year, the normal is that they will want to start finding a boyfriend or a girlfriend. And it usually happens by this girl telling this boy that this other girl likes him and she would like to go with him or the other way around.

Me: What is typical nowadays? It was a long time ago when I was in seventh and eighth grade and dating was, no, not until High School, tenth grade, eleventh grade. What do parents allow typical children to do?

Nancy: It's all different. It's all varied. Some parents are still adamant, this child is not going to go out on dates until they are 16. Some parents see them as old enough to start dating in Junior High and they allow them to even go out in a car.

Me: We are talking age 15 at the top right?

Nancy: Yes, 15 at the top. Some allow them to go only to school functions like the school dances with a boy, but nothing else. Most, boyfriend/girlfriend encounters take place in the hall, and that may go on for two days and then the next time it is somebody different.

Me: Do you counsel the boys too when it comes to sex ed? And what do you do?

Nancy: We have the abstinence classes here, which is a complete program. All of the boys and all of the girls go through it, and then I do some individual counseling. If I become aware of someone who is sexually active, sometimes they will come and share because they are worried about it. We definitely go into the health risks—sometimes I bring in my nurse, just depending on what action needs to be taken. Sometimes I go to parents depending on the situation.

Me: At this level there is not a privacy act or confidentiality act is there?

Nancy: Yes, there is. I try to handle that very carefully because they are not adults yet. I usually, maybe this comes with my old age, but I usually convince the child I'm working with that we have to contact parents.

Me: When they start in Junior High, are they looking towards High School, are they getting to the point where they start thinking about jobs yet? What is the typical progression of their interests advancing toward jobs and college?

Nancy: Here again it's different levels because all of them are maturing at such different stages. A lot of them still have unrealistic goals. A lot of my boys *know* they are going to be professional athletes. They *know* they are going to be making millions of dollars playing a sport. And I don't try to jerk that out from under them. But we do start homing in on more realistic goals. In Junior High it's more of a career awareness. We do the interest inventory so they understand the areas that they are truly interested in. I have kids who love school and want to keep going, and I have kids who hate school.

Me: Do they take this serious? I mean, do they listen to what you say?

Nancy: They do. In my career units they start a portfolio and put information into it, their learning style, their habits, their interests, their career path. In eighth grade, they basically do a sample for the High School plan, based on what they want to go into. It's not set in concrete but I try to teach them how to set up a four-year plan so that when they meet with the High School counselor they won't be overwhelmed.

Me: So you are showing them, this is your interest now, you have to have four years of High School to get there and this is where you start in ninth grade.

Nancy: That's exactly right. We take ninth to twelfth grade, and we say in this grade you will have to have this math, this class, etc. . . . and then at the end of eighth grade, they get with the High School counselors and make up their official four-year schedule.

Me: Briefly, do you remember all of the personality boxes we used to put ourselves into. We had introverts, extroverts, cliques, etc. . . . This may be a loaded question, because some autistics are also introverts, some extroverts, do you still categorize kids in your mind this way?

Nancy: I don't think we categorize them in our mind the way we used to, although believe me there still are those categories. We've kind of changed that to leaders and followers. We have a kid who we used to call extrovert showing high leadership skills who is out there wanting to be head of the student council, wanting to be in charge of this or that. Those we refer to as our school leaders, and then there are the followers, and it takes both to do anything. We can't accomplish anything unless we have some good followers to help implement a plan.

Me: When they hit seventh grade, do you see a change between the leaders and the followers? Do they just keep plodding along? Do some of the followers become leaders?

Nancy: That can happen, yes. I have seen it happen. I find that a lot of the kids who are really outgoing and want to be involved in everything are the leaders, but I have seen kids come over who have never been involved in anything, and all of a sudden get involved in one activity or a sport, and Boom! they just blossom and change totally. I feel every child needs to be involved in some organization or club activity in the school because that makes them feel a part of things and fulfills that need to belong. It also builds up their self-esteem. We can tell a kid every day they are great, but that is not going to do it. They have to have an accomplishment, and every time they feel they have succeeded, that's when the self-esteem comes up.

Me: Like in my seventh grade I was in the Geology Club. There were only six of us, but it was our interest and our little group.

Nancy: It left you with a good memory and made you feel like you belonged.

Me: Yes, and now we are back to the social…

Nancy: Yes, and that's where the social skills build up. Being with these groups no matter how small and doing these activities. The kids are just starting now. As they get on into High School there are going to be more activities, and I'm not saying they will have all successes with these experiences but there will still be a learning process and these activities will be filling an inner need.

Me: I think this is a good place to end. Is there anything you can tell me that is *so* typically Junior High? Have you covered everything?

Nancy: I think we've discussed everything. I think kids hit frustration sometimes easier at this age. This is simply because they have so much going on. They are dealing with a lot right now and frustration hits pretty easily. But hopefully we can help them with it. Along with what parents can deal with at home and at church or whatever, we can help them get through this. You know. They all survive and they all make great adults.

Me: We all live through Junior High, don't we?

Nancy: That's right. We all get through Junior High whether we like it or not. A lot of my eighth graders come to me and say, I don't want to go on to High School! But then once they get there they come back and say, we love it. That's another thing I always tell my sixth graders. They are going to like Junior High better than sixth grade, and my eighth graders are going to like High School better than Junior High. And they all kind of look at me and think, how can she say that? But that's what we want. Every school meets different needs because the student has different needs when they come to that school. I want all of my eighth graders to like High School better, and sixth graders Junior High. And a lot of them say, "I know I'm going to like it better because I won't have to walk in a line!"

Me: Ha! I never thought about that, but that's right! No more lines!

Nancy: No more lines and you know what that is? Showing that need for independence. No more standing in lines, they can just go. They love that!

Me: Which explains why seventh grade halls are so wild!

Nancy: Yes! But it's a teaching and a learning process. They are learning how to handle the non-structured situation. And every little thing has a purpose to help the kids grow, right down to the no lines.

I wonder if Jon, as Mark Twain writes, also thinks that his parents are ignorant right now?

chicken nugget #9

"Is there a lesson in these socks?"—dealing with tactile issues

...each man [read woman] reads his [her] own peculiar lessons according to his [her] own peculiar mind and mood.

(Herman Melville 1852)

Do I, as a parent of a child with a disability always have to "look on the bright side" and believe that "every cloud has its silver lining"?

Did you ever wonder who actually originated this silver lining? I have tried in vain to find the answer to this, an old English proverb was the closest I found and I also found it listed as a Portuguese proverb and French saying. Seems that several cultures wish to claim this silver. One thing I believe about the person who first said it, they lived in a climate that never suffered severe thunder storms, or tornadoes, and they knew nothing about raising a child with disabilities. Don't get me wrong, I didn't jump to this conclusion overnight—I've been contemplating this cloud with its silver lining ever since doing the laundry a while back.

On this particular Saturday, as I put white clothes into the washer I notice there are three of Jon's white socks that now have holes in them. "Why not an even pair?" is my first thought, which would make my life so much easier.

You see, wrapped up in Jon's autism, is something the experts call tactile defensiveness. In Mom and Dad terms this means *over* sensitive to touch. Not just touch from people, but the touch of objects against his skin. Objects like pillow-cases, tags in the back of t-shirts, long pants after wearing summer shorts, and socks.

I've always bemoaned the fact that we live in a state that has a full six months of winter. When it comes to Jon's tactile defensiveness, if he could live in sandals all year around, he would. He readily accepts the fact that during colder months he must switch back to wearing long pants, but when it comes to putting the socks back on, there is always a struggle. And it's not because his shoes may be too tight and the socks may pinch his toes. No. It's something much more complicated, which even Jon can't explain. The only explanation I get out of him is "Mom, they just don't *feel* right." So, unable to get any further, I try to understand.

Those socks, which look the same as all of the others in his drawer, and may have come out of the same package—just *don't feel right*.

Now you understand my disappointment when I find three of the good socks with holes clean through them. Not at the ankles, or toes, where they could be sewn up (maybe not, thread probably wouldn't feel right either), but holes at the ball of the foot, where all of his socks wear out. I drop the three socks in the trash, making a mental note that we will have to make one of our least favorite trips to the local department store to buy more socks.

Less than a week later, we are at the store, as Jon now has more days of the week left than pairs of socks in his drawer. As we stand in the sock aisle I try to wait patiently as Jon pokes his finger inside the corner of all the sock bags, trying to tell by his little poke if the socks will be good socks or bad socks. He finally narrows it down to two types, but can't seem to make up his mind. (Believe me when I say buying them both and taking them home and trying them out is not an option as I've been there too many times, and his cousins really don't like me shopping for them by giving them stuff Jon won't wear.) I glance over my shoulder and open a corner of one of the packages. I wiggle one lone sock out of the bag, make him sit down in the shoe aisle and put the sock on his foot. "Perfect!" he beams up at me.

Oh thank goodness! I didn't really want to open another bag! I stuff the sock into the bag and put them in the cart, making sure to grab another of the exact same kind. (When it works, double up!)

A week later I'm back in the laundry room and I find that fourth worn out sock, the mate of the guys that were thrown out the week before. Suddenly I set the sock down and think, "Is there a lesson in these socks?" Is there a lesson in the struggle my son goes through to find things that *feel right* to him? Is there a silver lining in the fact that something so simple as purchasing socks can be a big issue for Jon?

I drop the sock into the trash and slam the lid down on the washer in anger. NO!

There is no silver lining here. Some things are always going to be difficult for Jon. As he matures, it's true, the issues may change, but there will always be something in his life that he must overcome. Not just the normal issues that neurotypicals have like school, college, friends, dating, or jobs. Jon will have these issues plus more—like socks.

So as far as I'm concerned, there is no silver lining in the cloud of autism. I do not have to always look on the bright side and try to find meaning in every little act. There is no lesson in these socks, and I've spent entirely too much of my time trying to find one!

To borrow a phrase from another teenager I know—sometimes, life just sucks. So, get up, and get on with it. End of story.

Do we need to make our child's life comfortable every step of the way (literally), or do we need to teach him to learn to live with some discomfort?

Barnes & Noble Bookseller
1553 Almonesson Road
Deptford, NJ 08096
(856) 232-3123
05-14-07 S02891 R008

How to Be Yourself in a   14.95
9781843105046
Talking Teenagers: Infor   19.95
9781843108443
School Success for Kids   16.95
9781593632151

SUB TOTAL   51.85
SALES TAX   3.63
TOTAL   55.48
AMOUNT TENDERED
DEBIT CARD   55.48
CARD #:   ************3951
AMOUNT   55.48

TOTAL PAYMENT   55.48
      Thank you for Shopping at
      Barnes & Noble Booksellers
Shop online 24 hours a day www.bn.com
#49856 05-14-07 02:37P Jenn

You as the customer agree to pay the
above amount.
Thank you and come again!

Valid photo ID required for all returns, (except for credit card purchases) exchanges and to receive and redeem store credit. With a receipt, a full refund in the original form of payment will be issued for new and unread books and unopened music within 30 days from any Barnes & Noble store. For merchandise purchased with a check, a store credit will be issued within the first seven days. Without an original receipt, a store credit will be issued at the lowest selling price. With a receipt, returns of new and unread books and unopened music from bn.com can be made for store credit. Textbooks after 14 days or without a receipt are not returnable. Used books are not returnable.

Valid photo ID required for all returns, (except for credit card purchases) exchanges and to receive and redeem store credit. With a receipt, a full refund in the original form of payment will be issued for new and unread books and unopened music within 30 days from any Barnes & Noble store. For merchandise purchased with a check, a store credit will be issued within the first seven days. Without an original receipt, a store credit will be issued at the lowest selling price. With a receipt, returns of new and unread books and unopened music from bn.com can be made for store credit. Textbooks after 14 days or without a receipt are not returnable. Used books are not returnable.

Valid photo ID required for all returns, (except for credit card purchases) exchanges and to receive and redeem store credit. With a receipt, a full refund in the original form of payment will be issued for new and unread books and unopened music within 30 days from any Barnes & Noble store. For merchandise purchased with a check, a store credit will be issued within the first seven days. Without an original receipt, a store credit will be issued at the lowest selling price. With a receipt, returns of new and unread books

Chapter Ten

A bully by any other name is still a bully

When is teasing really bullying?

Imagine, if you will, a sixth grade child. She is the tallest in her class, and the first one to "develop" compared to her shorter, flat-chested girl-friends. This child is outgoing, friendly and very social, or she has been up to this point. But several things happen in sixth grade which affect this child. Besides the fact that she is the tallest girl in class, it seems that the boys have suddenly begun to notice her in a different way. Up to this point she was just one of the gang, playing with boys or girls, it didn't matter which. But now that she is in sixth grade, some of her little girl-friends have little boyfriends. Some of them are "going steady," a euphemism for not much at the age of 12, and her previously friendly friends who were boys, are now picking on her or teasing her.

This child is not a tattle tale; she has always been well liked by both girls and boys, so she doesn't understand why she is being picked on. She tries to ignore it. When a boy walks past her desk and shoves her books "accidentally" to the floor, she tries to pretend it didn't happen. The first time she comes back in from recess to find the entire contents of her desk tipped out onto the floor, she scurries to pick them up and says nothing. Then it happens a second time and a third.

One day she comes in from recess not only to find her desk dumped, but her purse dumped out all over the floor, her new feminine hygiene items strewn all over for everyone to see. The boys enter the classroom after her and a lot of snickering follows. This time the girl cannot help but get upset. She asks to speak to Mr. Johnson, her teacher, in the hall. She begins to cry as she tells him what has been going on, referring back to the previous incidents as well. Mr. Johnson, who is the first male teacher she has ever had, nods his head as he listens. Then he goes back into the room and asks, in front of the entire class, who is responsible for this? No one volunteers this information. He tells everyone that this teasing stops now. No one is to dump any more books or desks or purses.

A few days pass, and this girl gets laughed at, it's verbal teasing now. A few days later, she comes back in from recess to see that her desk has been moved all the way from its previous position to the far corner of the room. In fact it is next to the least popular student in the classroom. She gets the message. Because she told the teacher, the boys are relegating her to sit in the "unpopular" corner. This, after being friends with, and growing up with, most of these boys since kindergarten. She is not only upset, she is crushed. She is now one of the disliked—she is now a *they*, before she was a *we*.

Unfortunately from this day on, there is a change in this young girl's life. Where once she was outgoing, almost overly friendly, she grows painfully shy. Where once she felt that most kids were her friends, she feels friendless. And most importantly, when more books get shoved from her desk during the rest of the school year, this student learns that telling the teacher doesn't solve the problem but, in fact, can make it worse. She cries about it, but doesn't tell anyone. She ignores the teasing, the bullying, and can't wait until next year when they will all go to a larger school, Junior High, and surely life will be better.

This scenario illustrates the teasing and bulling of a neurotypical child. But what if this happens to a child with a disability such as autism?

At times in his life, Jon too has faced teasing from kids. When he was in elementary school there always seemed to be one student who had his number. One student who knew that Jon didn't like certain things, whether it was sounds, lights, songs, or habits. And once armed with this knowledge, this child then picked, teased, and pushed Jon until he was usually in tears. In elementary school we handled it by having the other child reprimanded, and Jon being told to try to ignore this obnoxious child. This worked, and to this day Jon refers to this boy as *wacky James*, the boy who always came after him on the playground.

A second situation, similar to this girl's story, happened to Jon in the sixth grade. For some reason, Jon developed an aversion to a song sung by a popular group at the time. If you knew the words, and heard them at unbearably loud decibels, you too may have developed a similar aversion. But, all too soon, it seemed there was a group of boys who knew that Jon hated this song with a passion. So they got a kick out of singing this song to him, in the hallways, in the cafeteria, or at recess, so that he would run away screaming. We tried to deal with this in a similar way to the previous incident, reprimanding the boys and trying to get Jon to realize that words really don't hurt.

This situation continued during the year until finally Jon gave one of these kids a shove. I got a call from the school that Jon was in tears in the principal's office and would be suspended for a day for fighting. (Our school district is a "no fight" school, meaning no exceptions.)

I arrived at school to take my crying child home. Yes, he knew he had done wrong, but "Mom, that kid just wouldn't stop it," he said. We dealt with the suspension at home by taking away his computer games for a week. I also passed out the book *Asperger Syndrome and Rage* by Brenda Smith Myles, so that all of the IEP team members could read it. She gives an excellent example of a behavior contract, that Jon's teachers were able implement and fill out with him. It lists step by step, choices and consequences, which the students have to fill in themselves, and honestly, after this was done there were no more problems, that we saw, the rest of the year.

Jon experienced minor teasing in seventh grade, but I was told this was all typical Junior High kid stuff, and Jon needed to learn to deal with it.

Then we came to eighth grade. Since the beginning of the school year, there were certain kids who had once again begun singing this song at Jon. As always, we told him to ignore it. He did. Then we told him to play along with the kids and act like he was the conductor. So he tried that. Then one day as he was waiting for lunch to be over he had a particularly horrendous time in the hall, and when he came home he told me everyone hated him.

I then did what any parent would do, I spoke to the caseworker, who again told me that this was normal Junior High stuff, and Jon needed to learn to deal with it. But I wanted to know how? How was my autistic son, who took every little thing and made it into something big, going to learn to handle this teasing?

I went from the caseworker to the school counselor, who knew all about teasing, and who could hopefully tell me if this was teasing or bullying, and how did "typical" children learn to handle it? After our talk she suggested Jon come and talk to her and they would outline some strategies.

A few days later I got a call from the counselor, telling me that Jon had stopped in to see her and they now had a plan on how to deal with the boys who were picking on him. She felt that things would be okay and that Jon was trying to handle things himself.

At this same time I began to get notes written by Jon's aide in his daily communications notebook that Jon was reacting inappropriately to kids teasing him. Jon was poking, shoving, and name-calling. He was getting into trouble for this, and at home we went over and over the proper responses that he was supposed to be making to these kids.

Alas, things came to a halt when I got the inevitable call from the principal's office. Jon was in trouble for kicking a kid underneath the table. The interesting thing was that Jon admitted that this kid hadn't done anything, but in Jon's mind, he anticipated what this tormentor was going to say and decided to kick him before it happened. (Even if it gets him into more trouble, if pushed for the truth, Jon tells it.) The principal explained all of this to me over the phone, and told me Jon was given an hour of in-school suspension, in the middle of the day.

Later, when I picked Jon up from school, I asked him what had happened. Yes, he admitted, this time the kid hadn't said anything, but this kid had sang at him just the day before, and he expected it to happen again, so he kicked him under the table *before* he could do it. He also told me he *loved* detention. It was nice and quiet and he was able to get his homework done.

This time I went in to speak directly to the principal. I wanted to know why these same kids were still bullying Jon? In my mind, almost daily teasing now equates to bullying, and I wanted to know why these kids were allowed to sit next to my son if they were constantly at each other?

During this meeting I learned that the principal had not been made aware of the fact that certain kids were constantly the ones teasing or, in my words, *bullying* my son. Up to my meeting with him, he didn't have any names to go by and only knew that Jon was behaving inappropriately. He was totally unaware that Jon and I felt these kids were bullying him because they sang this song at him on a daily basis.

The principal assured me that he would look into it and see that these kids were brought into his office and told to leave Jon alone. We also discussed the fact that perhaps in-school detention was not a good punishment for Jon since he felt that detention was a safe haven, because of the peace and quiet in the room. I left this meeting confident that the problem would be, if not solved, looked in to.

Once again, I carried in the book *Asperger Syndrome and Rage* and asked that those teachers working with Jon would read it and realize why he reacts the way he does when he is being bullied.

The next day, the principal and I spoke again. Both boys had been brought into the office, both admitting that yes, they had probably been teasing Jon too much. They were apologetic and wouldn't do it again.

A week later I received another call, this time from the assistant principal as the principal was out of the building. Jon had raised his hand in class to say that a kid was aggravating him and had done the right thing by asking to leave the room. However, on the way out the door, he punched the kid in the arm. Jon was being suspended for the rest of the day, and the next, for fighting.

When I arrived at school to pick him up, again he was in tears. He said that the same boy who he had been having trouble with was singing at him and humming this same song at him under his breath. He said first that he had karate chopped the kid's arm, but then admitted that he had punched him with a closed fist. The assistant principal was very patient with him and explained that he was being suspended for fighting. I was okay with this suspension, but I was angry that this same kid was still bullying, and in my mind now harassing my son.

On the way to my son's locker he told me, "Mom, I want to die. Nobody likes me." My heart broke for him. Yes, I know. A lot of *normal* Junior High School kids express these same feelings during these difficult years, but this was my *autistic* son, a young man who gets upset when I kill a fly in the house instead of escorting it out the door. He had been harassed to the point of punching someone and now wanting to die.

At that moment an unfortunate thing happened as we were heading out of the building. The teacher who had written Jon up for punching stopped me in the hall. She explained that she was the one who had sent him to the principal's office. I said, that was okay, but from now on would you please separate these two kids? This was the same kid who had been constantly pushing Jon's buttons by singing at him and who Jon had said a few days before had told him, "I enjoy bullying you."

This teacher replied that she hated to tell me this, but this boy was three seats away from Jon and he hadn't done a thing to him. I told her if Jon was pushed for the truth, he told the truth and that she was mistaken because Jon was able to imitate this boy's humming this particular song under his breath. She said, she didn't appreciate me raising my voice at her! (Yes, I had raised my voice, as she stood there and told me in so many words that my son was a liar and that this boy hadn't been harassing Jon at all.) At this point, I quickly clamped my mouth shut, turned about face, and left.

But not before I parked my son on a chair and went back into the principal's office. I confessed to the assistant principal that unfortunately I had just gone off on one of his teachers, because she had told me that this kid had *not* been doing anything and that Jon had punched him for no reason. Thank goodness for his patience, as he assured me once again, they would look into it. The next day, Jon was suspended and we made him go to work with us and be bored, so he would realize he was being punished. The first call I got that day was from the teacher who I had yelled at in the hallway. She was calling to tell me that she was surprised to find out that this other boy had lied to her. There were several witnesses to the fact that he was indeed humming this particular song at Jon and that he had been picking on Jon for some time. She was calling to tell me that they had reprimanded him for lying and that Jon was telling the truth. (I wanted to say, "well duh?" But I bit my tongue!) We spoke for a few more minutes and I was waiting for her to offer an apology. When she ended by saying, "Well, I have to get back to class," I realized an apology wasn't coming, but I did thank her for calling.

The second phone call was from the principal telling me that this boy had been disciplined and as far as he could assure me, neither boy would be bullying Jon any more.

The next day, Jon went back to school.

Was school wonderful and rosy after that? No. But the speech teacher who was working on social skills with Jon began role-playing with him, so if he was being harassed, he was forced to come up with a good conflict resolution. And the principal decided to let Jon out of his classes a few minutes early to see if he could get to the next class without having to deal with anyone singing at him along the way.

I too had several long conversations after that. One with the principal requesting that these two boys not be allowed near Jon, or Jon near them, for the rest of the year, and asking that the boys' parents be informed about the situation. I had another with the Special Services Autism Coordinator for the district. She hadn't been told about the entire situation, the caseworker had not passed on the incidents or our concerns. I felt she needed to be aware of every detail, in case it happened yet again.

The last conversation was a conference call with our family attorney and the director of the local Disabilities Board for our county. What we talked about was the fact that this bullying could be considered harassment, and if I needed to do something more, for example have an attorney write a letter for me to the school district, we should do so. (We've decided to wait on that since the minute an attorney enters an IEP meeting or even sends a letter, all doors of communication close.)

I had one more important conversation—with Jon. The evening before he was getting ready to go back to school I managed to hug him on his way through the kitchen. With him being 14 *and* autistic, I have to grab hugs when I can. I told him I was very proud of him, for handling all of this so well. And I reminded him that when he was younger he was suspended for fighting, and had learned from that experience, and things had gotten better. I told him he would learn from this experience, and next year he would be in High School and things would be different. (Notice I didn't guarantee better. I'm always afraid that my words will come back to haunt me.)

After actually allowing me to hug him he said, "Yes, but, when I was little I pushed and kicked kids for no reason at all." This was the way he remembered those events I guess. I said, "Yes, but now you are hitting for a reason, and you can't do that either. You just have to learn how to react differently."

I thought, but didn't say to him, I was so proud of the fact that he did stick up for himself, and after finally getting tired of this kid, he told the teacher and asked to leave the room. Even the fact that he punched the kid on the way out the door, shows that he is sticking up for himself in a very typical Junior High kind of way. Jon just doesn't have the common sense not to do it in front of a teacher like the majority of the students!

The same week Jon was suspended my "quote a day" calendar had this one by Harvey Fierstein: "Never be bullied into silence. Never allow yourself to be made a victim. Accept no one's definition of your life: define yourself." Amazing coincidence!

I read this and immediately thought about the girl I described at the beginning of this chapter. How I wish someone had told this sixth grade girl, who happened to be me, "Never be bullied into silence." When I had finally told the teacher what was happening, things got worse instead of better. I lived in misery for the rest of my sixth grade year. I was being bullied, I was afraid to tell the teacher again, and I soon began to think it was *my* fault that I was being picked on.

I allowed myself to be made a victim, but I refuse to allow my son to do the same. Yes, my son happens to be autistic, but between the two of us, we will not be bullied into silence.

Sheila Wagner, Assistant Director at the Emory Autism Center in Atlanta, writes about how to support an autistic student who is being bullied: "Accept that bullying occurs, believe the student with AS, make sure they have at least one supportive friend and teacher they can count on, teach skills that can deflect bullying, do not have proximity to bullies and have real consequences for the bullies" (Wagner 2004, p.25). How I wish I would have had these instructions during Jon's eighth grade year. I feel that if I hadn't waited so long, and let the teachers convince me that this was just "normal Junior High teasing," perhaps Jon wouldn't have punched a kid and gone through suspension. I didn't have those words of advice, but you do!

If Jon had not gone through this, he would not have learned the consequences of punching—how do I learn to let him learn, no matter what?

chicken nugget #10

When parents hit a brick wall in communication

If life is just a bowl of cherries, where can I get a bowl of those?

Most of our experiences with our son and his school have been very positive but once in a while communication breakdown does occur, and when this happens, life is not a bowl of cherries!

Eighth grade was the most difficult time for Jon. There were kids picking on him and it seemed that a few of the educators working with him were experiencing "burnout." Our breakdown came towards the second half of the year, on a Saturday when the kids were required to go a half-day to make up for a snow day. (It's a mid-western thing, and doesn't make sense to the parents either!) I picked Jon up from school and took him back to the office with me. While there I opened my e-mail to find a letter from one of the educators working with him. The letter began with her concerns for Jon's comprehension in reading. She had given him a quick reading and computer test that morning and he had scored poorly. Next, she pointed out that in math he still used his fingers as a visual aide which was not a good sign. Then she asked in a tone I hadn't heard from her before, "Don't you want your son to live up to his intellectual potential?" She went on to suggest that he work with flash cards for math, watch the History Channel to improve his vocabulary, read a book at home every night, and learn to stop using his fingers. Otherwise, he would be experiencing serious problems very soon.

I remember sitting with my mouth open as I re-read the e-mail almost hearing the snippy attitude coming through her comments. She was asking *us*, probably the most overly concerned parents at the school, if we wanted Jon to live up to his intellectual potential or not? Exactly where was this coming from? Did she forget which parent she was addressing here?

I read the e-mail to my husband and he heard anger in her voice. "What has gotten into her?" he asked. I didn't know, but I planned on finding out.

One good thing, or possibly bad, about e-mail is that you can respond immediately to a person's words. So I did. In the heat of the moment I sent her an e-mail explaining the she should know by now that his reading comprehension level has always been connected to his interest level, more so than normal kids. If Jon wasn't interested in the topic he was reading, he just would not pay attention as he read. (I had asked Jon what he had read for her and he said something about Rome? He didn't even remember what the short piece had been about.) I also pointed out that he had just finished reading Tolkien's *Lord of the Rings* because he was so interested in it, and wasn't this High School reading level? Then I addressed the math problem and reminded her that he was a visual learner and used visual prompts. I too had seen him doing strange things with his fingers in math, but he was well able to do long division, all multiplication problems, and beginning algebra and geometry. Why did we want to take away his visual prompt for math if it was working for him? I also did strange things with the point of my pencil when I was adding a long column of figures. Yes, we don't want others to laugh at him, so we should slowly try to get him away from looking at his fingers, but let's not take away a visual that was working for him.

After addressing these two issues, I asked if he was falling behind in reading and math? Did we need to have an IEP meeting the next week to address these issues and write them into his IEP for the rest of the year? And if he was having problems, why was I just now hearing about them?

By this time the keyboard was steaming, and so was I. I sent my reply and carbon copied it to the Special Services Autism Coordinator, also attaching this teacher's original e-mail to me.

I immediately got a response telling me no, an IEP meeting wasn't necessary right now and yes, she realized his reading comprehension was always based on interest. She said she "guessed" counting on his fingers wouldn't harm him for life (not her exact words, but that's what I heard), and she was just trying to give us a heads-up, but not to worry, he was not behind in either subject.

I read her response and was just as confused as when I had received the first e-mail. Then what was this about? If all of these were really non-issues and just her trying to give us a heads-up, why send me this e-mail asking whether I wanted Jon to live up to his intellectual potential? I copied this response, and sent it on to the autism coordinator, along with the line, "Any ideas where *any* of this is coming from?"

What happened? Not much. Did I ever find out what really prompted this condescending e-mail from an educator who has worked on and off with Jon since he was first diagnosed?—No.

The following week I did get a call from the Director of Special Services for the Schools. She too had gotten copies of the e-mails. What did she say?

Basically the only thing she said was that if I ever wished to call an IEP meeting, it was well within my rights. (I knew that of course.) However, I think her main worry was that this teacher had responded that a meeting wasn't necessary. When I attempted to ask her about these e-mails from the previous week, she changed the subject. She said she just wanted me to know that they *all* had Jon's best interest at heart, and that we were *all* on the same page.

The next day I got a call from the autism coordinator. She actually agreed with me that these e-mails came from nowhere, and she had no further explanation. She too changed the subject and we talked about next year's High School schedule.

Did I hear anything more from this teacher? We did work with her the rest of the year, but I must admit that the communication had already broken down. This breakdown was also passed down to my son's aide. My husband suggested that teachers were perhaps experiencing burnout? The jury is still out, as far as I'm concerned.

However, things were not the same the rest of the school year. Because of this one morning of condescending/angry e-mails, we barely survived the rest of the year with these two people. My husband's stabilizer was to keep repeating, "School is almost over, let's hang in there until next year, different school, different educators." This worked for him, but what kept *me* from pulling my hair out the rest of the year?

I remember crying on my sister's shoulder. She has taught school for 20 years and is my support. I read her these e-mails, and her comment was that this teacher was way off base and should have been called on the carpet. I also remember going for a drive one day and crying in frustration while I was out in the country and no one was around to see or hear me.

But what worked best for me, was a practice I had developed while at graduate school. Public writing is notorious for feeling like you are laying your guts out on the table and allowing others, teachers and fellow students, to stomp all over them. So while in school, to keep my sanity and keep from beating myself up, I practiced the following visualization technique. Whenever I would hear the echo of any negative comments in my head from class, a critique group, or comments written on my papers, I would take those thoughts and visualize a mason jar—you know, the kind grandma sealed with wax and put jellies and preserves in. I would visualize that person or those written comments inside that jar, and I would put the lid on them, right down to sealing it with wax.

Suddenly, I couldn't hear the negative in my head any more, and I was able to move on. This may sound strange, but I've heard of other people writing down thoughts that bother them, down on actual paper and setting a match to it. My technique was a lot faster, less time-consuming, and more cost-effective.

Thus, this is how I kept my sanity the rest of the year. I put those two educators in their own little jars, along with all of those e-mails. I felt bad that communication, after so many good years, had broken down, but I also realized that sometimes you can't go back and fix it, you just have to move forward.

I learned that sometimes you do lose your sense of humor, and no matter how hard you try, it won't come back. Even now, I have to force myself not to get angry over this situation again. I had to decide whether to include this chapter, and opted to write it to show that even when things are working, they can suddenly not work, and sometimes we, who are only human, may make things worse. Parents aren't perfect, but neither are teachers.

So what do we do? Put those negative thoughts behind us and quote Abraham Lincoln, who said, "This too shall pass."

Anyone can make a big mistake, but how do we keep from then becoming overcautious?

Chapter Eleven

An interview with an expert on autism—Dr. B.J. Freeman

What should a parent of an autistic youth do?

Dr. B.J. Freeman is a retired Professor of Medical Psychology at the University of California, Los Angeles. In *Parent to Parent* I featured her list on evaluating and questioning treatment programs. I interview her here to ask an expert's opinion on what a parent of an autistic youth should do.

Me: What is the first thing you would tell a parent they ought to do when facing a diagnosis of autism or Asperger's Syndrome for the first time?

Dr. Freeman: The first thing a parent should always do is do not panic. We have learned a lot about ASDs and Asperger's Syndrome. Children with ASDs will and can get better over time. ASD is best viewed now as a social communication learning disability. Some people have trouble learning to read, some people have trouble learning to do math, our children have trouble learning social communication skills. However, with appropriate intervention and intensive help our children can become happy, productive members of society and live independently.

Me: What ought they not do?

Dr. Freeman: Parents should not rush into decisions regarding treatment. It is very important to become informed and educated. Parents know their child better than anyone else. While there is much controversy about what constitutes appropriate programming, parents need to be able to evaluate all the information. I also recommend that parents identify a professional who they can talk to about the different options, someone who remains open but is willing to help guide parents as the "captain of the ship."

Me: Where ought parents go for current, accurate information and why?

Dr. Freeman: Again parents should identify a professional who is knowledgeable about information about the current theories of autism spectrum disorder. It is important to establish a collaborative relationship with someone who has an open mind, but who can help parents honestly evaluate the claims made by many treatments.

Me: Where ought they not look for information and why?

Dr. Freeman: Becoming educated as a parent of a child with ASD is absolutely critical. Probably the most inaccurate information can be found on the internet. Conversely, the internet also has some of the best information about ASD. Therefore, having someone who can help parents evaluate the information is much more important than where the information is obtained.

Me: What are the important steps parents ought to take when working with educators at the elementary school level?

Dr. Freeman: The most important thing a parent can do is to establish a collaborative working relationship with the school. Having a team approach is what all children benefit from, and this is true of elementary school, Junior High School, and High School. All members of the team do not always have to agree, but it should be a total collaborative team approach. We have always had a good team and have really only had problems about 10–15 percent of the time.

Me: What about medications?

Dr. Freeman: Medications should always be used with caution. If the behavior occurs in only one situation, medication is not the answer. Medication should only be tried after a systematic behavior program has been in place and found not to work. In trying medication it is important to find a doctor who understands both autism spectrum disorders and medications, as our children do not always respond to medication appropriately. Again, it is important to have a collaborative relationship with both the school and the physician in order to ascertain if the medication is appropriate for the child.

Me: What ought parents expect as a prognosis as their child with autism/Asperger's grows older?

Dr. Freeman: Every child with ASD is of course different. However, I talk to parents about keeping their expectations as high as possible, or as one parent once said to me, I keep my hopes extremely high, but my expectations a little bit lower. Having ASD or Asperger's is not an excuse not to engage in tasks. For example, "I cannot do my homework today because I feel a little autistic," is not an acceptable response. Understanding why children with autism have difficulty with certain tasks, such as initiation, motivation, organization and independence, is absolutely critical to understanding the child. However, if we do not expect the child with autism to develop, grow and learn, become independent and a functional member of society, it will not happen.

Me: What are the chances that my autistic/Asperger's child could live independently on a day-to-day basis?

Dr. Freeman: As noted above, if we push the child to develop functional skills, the probabilities are very high that the child can live independently. We have learned a lot about ASD. Early intensive intervention makes a huge difference in terms of outcome. Teaching children the practical day-to-day skills that will help them be functional in the community becomes an absolute mandatory part of an educational program. I talk to parents about asking yourself, when writing IEP goals, is this a goal that will help my child be independent? If you cannot answer that question in the affirmative, then we need to move on. It is important to understand that ASD children do not always use the skills that they have. Therefore, it is important to focus not on skills such as will they be able to do calculus, but will they be able to make change and be independent. If we focus on those skills and they are taught in a specific way, then our children have a great increased probability of living independently.

Me: Ought a parent plan for no marriages or grandchildren involving this child?

Dr. Freeman: Children with ASD should have the same expectations and opportunities as anyone else. We have increasing evidence that people with ASD are marrying and having children. That should be an extremely individual choice, and we hope for each person with ASD to be able to make the choice that is relevant to them. What is important is that we help our children be able to make a distinction between being lonely and needing time to be alone, and our job as parents and advocates is to make sure when a person with autism is an adult they can make those decisions.

Me: What is the final bit of advice you would give a parent?

Dr. Freeman: The final bit of advice is don't focus always on the child's disabilities. You need to spend a great deal of time focusing on a child's *abilities*, looking to help children with autism spectrum disorders find their niche in life. For many of our higher-functioning children getting them through High School with their ego intact becomes our primary responsibility. Once out of High School it is much easier to find their niche in society. It is also important never to give up hope for our children. While it is important to be realistic, it is also important to have high hopes and expectations for our children no matter where they are functioning on the spectrum.

What will I do when I don't *find an expert to answer future questions about my son?*

Literally speaking

Rodale's *Synonym Finder* expands the word *literal* as "word-for-word, verbatim, accurate, exact, precise, strict, undeviating, matter-of-fact, obtuse, blunt, and authentic." I read through all of these terms with Jon in mind, my literal-thinking son.

When he was younger it used to be the idioms he didn't understand. "Cat got your tongue," "Let sleeping dogs lie," and so on. Now that he is older, he gets those, and even laughs and jokes about them. But he is still just as much of a literal thinker as he ever was.

A few weeks back we had an argument. He got upset over something small, something we couldn't do anything about, and I got upset with him for getting so upset over something so trivial. He cried, I raised my voice, you can fill in the blanks.

A while later, he was still upset with me. So I apologized for raising my voice and tried to explain to him why I had gotten upset with him. He was able to tell me that sometimes he hated me when I yelled at him. And sometimes he felt like his thoughts were going to take over and a very evil person was going to come out.

I mulled this over for a few minutes, remembering times when I had felt the same way about my parents during my teenage years, and tried to decide how to answer. Then I explained to him that those angry thoughts he had about me didn't make him an evil person.

He said that he felt he might go to (he pointed at the floor, meaning hell) because of these thoughts.

I said, "Well, are you sure there is a *down there?* No one has ever been there and come back to tell us about it."

He recounted that the two summers he had gone to church camp, they had told him that the story of the Bible and the devil was a real story.

I now carefully pondered how to answer this one. Yes, I have a strong faith in God, but did I want my son to see my point or just continue to take things so literally? I opted for, excuse the expression, playing the devil's advocate. "Yes, I know there are a lot of people who believe that way. But you really don't know 100 percent for sure that those stories are true. It's called believing them by faith. Meaning we might not have facts, or proof, but we believe them."

He seemed to be calming down, and getting over his upset, so I continued. "And you know, there is no evil side of you, waiting to come out. You are not an evil person when you have bad thoughts. You are just Jon, a kid, having a bad thought because you are angry about something."

He suddenly sighed with relief. "Really...no evil person inside me," he repeated. "I didn't realize that."

"No, you are just a kid who gets angry sometimes. That evil person living inside someone is just a story like on *Dexter's Laboratory* where the evil Dexter comes out. It's all fiction."

He immediately stopped crying and his thoughts seemed to connect to something else, because he said, "I think there are many gods out there. You know, many names for many gods?"

I told him that this was a possibility. I believed that there was *one* God with many names. He said, yes, he could see that too.

I then took this opportunity to give him a short lesson in thinking literally, explaining again how life was not black and white (a lesson we go through quite often), and how sometimes you should just stay in the middle of the road and not be so literal.

He listened, I think he got some of it.

But soon I found myself re-teaching that same lesson. It's the day after the elections. My candidate hasn't won. (Alas, life goes on and it isn't the first time!) I wake Jon up for school and tell him, "Well, my candidate didn't win, I guess we are moving to Canada."

He slowly wakes up and says, "We are moving to Canada?"

I quickly retract that and tell him, no, it's a joke, only an expression, because my candidate didn't win. He shrugs and heads towards the shower, and I think, there I go again, confusing my son.

On the way out the door for school I remind him that although it's raining he doesn't have to put his hood up on his jacket, it will mess up his hair. He picks his backpack up and puts it on his back. His dad tells him, you don't have to wear it into the car! And we both laugh as he ignores us both, pulling his hood up too.

On the way to school I explain to him what a literal thinker is. Someone who thinks idioms are true, like "Cat got your tongue," someone who because they are wearing a shirt with buttons thinks that all the buttons need to be buttoned up. If they are wearing a jacket with a hood, the hood must go up. If they are carrying a backpack, the backpack must go on, because it goes on the back. He laughs as he realizes I'm joking and talking about him.

"You are a literal thinker, you know?"

"Yeah," he says.

"But remember, this also has to do with what I always tell you too. Life is not all black and white, there is some gray. You sometimes need to just stay in the middle of the road. Don't take everything so literally."

"Yeah, okay."

He gets out of the car in the pouring rain and I hand him his art paper he is supposed to carry in that morning. He had to iron a paper bag the night before, to remove all wrinkles for this project. I tell him, "Here you go, try not to wrinkle it."

As I look out the rearview mirror, he is gingerly carrying it in the pouring rain towards the door. Hmmm, I think. Maybe I should have stated that differently? "Hurry inside, but don't wrinkle the paper?"

I picture this one in my mind—he runs across the street through the rain, tries not to wrinkle the paper, and bulldozes over a few dawdling kids.

Okay, I concede. If I want my son to stop taking things so literally, then I obviously need to speak to him a little differently. How about; "Try to hurry inside, don't run, don't knock into anyone and try not to wrinkle the paper, but it's okay if gets wrinkled, it's not the end of the world. And by the way, love you and have a great day!" Okay, I meant that last part to be taken *literally!*

Chapter Twelve

Choosing your battles
Fighting the system

You've got to know when to hold 'em, and know when to fold 'em.

(Poker players' credo)

I realize I am my son's advocate, but how do I know when to stand up for him and when to shut up?

High School begins, whether we like it or not. It will be different for Jon I know, and different for us too. High School is supposed to be all about independence and breaking away from your parents. But how do we balance that when we have been our son's advocates for such a long time? I've always been his voice. How do I teach him to be his own voice?

When Jon was first diagnosed and we were getting to know our way around in the world of autism, IEP meetings, and special services, I remember having long pre-meeting discussions with my husband. We knew we had to work with the school system—living in a very small town, you only have one school to attend, unlike larger communities where you may be able to transfer into another—and we knew the best way to attract bees was with honey. (Trust me, the analogy fits.) As a result, very early, although we didn't understand autism, or the system, we learned how to work it. It—*the System*.

Before every IEP meeting I would type up our agenda, what *we* were concerned about and what *we* needed to have answered. I would also try to end on a positive note and write questions specifically asking about Jon's progress. Don't get me wrong, I knew Jon's teachers had their own meeting agenda, but I always tried to incorporate ours into theirs. I would type up these questions, concerns, or thoughts, and along with any new information I had found, I would make copies for every educator who would be attending the meeting. When I first started doing this, I was met with looks of surprise, but mostly I was graciously received. Several times I was told that it was nice to have a parent in a meeting who had their thoughts organized, and who was willing to go the extra mile in finding and providing information to help teachers work with a student.

But every once in a while, when there was something on our agenda which perhaps they weren't going to agree with, or we felt was very critical in Jon's education, we learned we had to work things a little differently, and we quickly learned the *good-cop-bad-cop* routine. One cop plays bad and threatens or roughs up the suspect, trying to get information out of him. The other cop plays good, defends the suspect against the bad cop and succeeds in gaining trust, and information, from him.

During our pre-meeting discussions, I would read our notes to my husband and we would decide how to play it. I was always the bad cop, asking for things, pointing out our wishes, suggesting change, and he would come along, joke with them, get them to relax, and be the good cop.

Do I feel this was, or is, dishonest? At first I did, because we were consciously deciding how to get the system to work for us. But then my husband, who has been in sales his entire life, explained to me that we were really just using a sales technique. Often he said, when you want a person to do something, you manipulate them in some way. He assured me it is no different than realizing you catch more bees with honey. I was trying to catch Jon's teachers, my husband was there, spreading the honey. And this worked—at least 90 percent of the time.

But what about the other 10 percent? What did we do when it wasn't working? When we weren't able to get what we wanted?—We learned to choose our battles.

One of the first battles we chose to fight after Jon's diagnosis was for a classroom paraprofessional aide. Jon needed someone with him so that he would be able to survive in the regular classroom. As a result, he was given an aide in first grade and has always had one. Over the years the aide's role has changed considerably, and now in ninth grade we are diligently working on removing the aide, for Jon's own good. The aide went from being with him 100 percent of the day to just being available in his classroom. The aide has gone from helping him try to talk to peers, to standing back, observing, and later giving him ideas on what he could have done differently. Depending on who has been working with him, this aide has, at times, gone from friend to foe.

One of his aides, during the terrible Junior High years actually became quite negative about him by the time her "tour of duty" was over. We tried not to take this personally. Junior High was a very difficult time, and my husband stated at one of our IEP meetings that he realized "everyone gets burnt out." We decided when this aide started taking Jon's curtness as rudeness and his to-the-point comments personally, and getting her "feelings" hurt, that she had been working with him too long and had forgotten that this was part of autism! Thank goodness our school has always had a policy that the aides don't work with the same student too many years in a row.

Another battle we insisted on fighting was the school assembly battle. When Jon was first diagnosed he was in first grade and refused to be in the large gymnasium where all school assemblies were taking place. We wrote into his IEP that he would have an option of wearing head-phones we had purchased for him, or he could leave the assembly and go somewhere else. Overall, this has worked, sometimes he sits through them, sometimes he gets upset at the noise level and leaves. So at the beginning of High School, when I was told that there would be a Spirit Assembly the first week, I immediately contacted his caseworker. I explained to her that this was what Jon usually did in the past, and that since the entire purpose of this assembly was to see how loud the students could get, he would need to have the same options available to him.

For some reason as I was explaining what he had done before, gone to the library, or somewhere quiet during assembly, she interrupted me and said, "Oh, the library is not an option. The school will be locked." At that moment I saw red and said I would have to call her back. Then I placed a call to the autism coordinator and told her what the situation was. I repeated my previous conversation, saying that I had been told that this was no longer an option for Jon. She patiently listened to me and said she would look into it.

I stewed over it for two more days before the assembly, preparing to fight this battle, the bad cop in me coming out, when she called me back. She said she had spoken to the caseworker and somehow I had misun-derstood. The library wasn't an option, but they did have a plan where

Jon could go to her classroom and sit and do homework with the aide if he needed to leave the assembly. She suggested that perhaps this hadn't been explained to me thoroughly.

Boy, did I feel dumb. I had jumped to a wrong conclusion, and the only explanation I had was that the previous year in Junior High we had fought so many battles that already I was anticipating a problem with the High School when there wasn't one. The next day when I was picking Jon up from school I was able to catch his caseworker in the hallway and apologize for not listening to her, and I groveled a little too. Groveling I learned from my husband, the good cop.

But what about other battles that I've consciously chosen *not* to fight? Like the one with the music director in sixth grade? Jon was interested in learning to play an instrument, any instrument, although he didn't know which yet. We attended the parents' night with the music director and his assistants. Jon looked over all of the choices and chose either percussion or flute. Being a flautist, who hadn't played since college, I encouraged him toward the percussion. I felt that flute playing required too much multitasking, breathing, finger movement, note reading, which Jon didn't have. In addition he had an uncanny knack for keeping the beat. All of the choir directors had noticed this during music class. He couldn't carry a pitch, but he sure had the beat.

We filled out the forms requesting percussion for the following sixth grade year. Imagine our disappointment when we were told at the beginning of the year that there were only so many percussion spots that could be filled, and Jon hadn't been given one of them. I dropped by the school on the day the teachers had meetings and left the director's assistant a packet of information about high-functioning autism and about trying to work with Jon's interests in developing his skills, such as his ability to keep a rhythm.

A few days later I called and spoke with her, explaining who I was and telling her that due to Jon's autism we felt this would be a perfect place for him and perhaps he would find his niche in the band in the back row, percussion. She listened to me and explained again that there were no other openings but maybe trombone? I asked her if she had read the information I had put in her mailbox. "No," she said, "But I did get it." My thoughts at that moment? I was very angry, and wondered why did they give kids a choice on the instrument they wished to play, only to turn them down. I told her I would talk to my husband and get back to her.

School started, and Jon was placed in study hall, not band. I was furious, and ready to go head to head with this lady band assistant. I was ready to fight this battle and get him into the band no matter what. But then several things happened.

That year, sixth grade, we put Jon in an inclusion classroom without a paraprofessional aide. This meant that he would be in a class that had a team teacher, and about five or six other students who had IEPs. Our school district has at least one inclusion classroom per grade, and we thought this would help get Jon away from depending on an aide. Both of his teachers and his caseworker contacted me about the band issue and suggested it was possibly a good thing that Jon hadn't gotten into the band since the team teacher did her re-teaching and tutoring with these students during study hall, and band students didn't have study hall.

The other thing that happened was I read an article in the local paper about the band. Being a small school, we had one band director and two assistants. This director traveled between High School and Junior High, and taught six different ages of students. Not only this, but he had taken his High School band to the state championship the year before and had garnered top honors both in symphonic and marching band. What this told me was: one, this guy was good, and two, he was serious. He had few spots open in his band not because he was stingy, but because he only wanted serious band students. Perhaps putting Jon into this very competitive situation, even if it was only percussion, was not a good idea.

So, I let this one go. I let the teachers talk me into the fact that he would be better off in study hall during that hour, and I didn't go after the director's assistant and chew her up for her lack of understanding of Jon's situation.

Jon was disappointed he didn't make it into the band and went on to do okay in the inclusion classroom and study hall. But the very next year, he was placed with an aide again. It seemed that the team teaching didn't work with Jon because the other teacher was soon acting as Jon's aide, they said, and was possibly neglecting her other students. Yes. I could see how this would happen. How can one person be the aide for five or six students, all with IEPs? This had never made much sense to me.

Did I regret not fighting this battle over the band?—Not until recently.

At the beginning of High School, for Jon's English class, they were asked to write a short essay pretending to look back on their High School years from college. When he brought the half-started essay home to finish, I saw that Jon started his paper out by saying that he should have been in the band. Immediately I was flooded with guilt. I asked him to explain further, and he said he wanted to be in the band because he wanted to be a conductor. Okay, I wondered where this came from. He further explained that it would be fun to be able to control the sounds in the band, the noise level and who plays what. I began to understand. He wasn't really in love with playing a musical instrument, but he had seen the strength and control a conductor has when they conduct a band.

Next in his essay he said, as he pretended to look back from college, that he should have been in sports. Once again I asked him to explain. Because you can be a part of a team, but I wouldn't want to be hurt while playing, he added.

As he wrote through this essay, I learned that he did have things he wished he had done, band, sports, but when I pressed him to see if he really wanted to do those things and why, his reasons weren't logical, they were Jon-logical. Most importantly, when I told him it wasn't too late, he could still do both, but to be a band director, you had to play several instruments and be able to read music, he said, "No, no, never mind. I want to draw and do computer animation. I want to be like Walt Disney." Which is how he concluded his essay.

Over the years there have been other battles I chose not to fight. Some of them, like the band issue, I look back and think perhaps I should have. Others, I've forgotten and they don't keep circling in my brain, which means I was probably right at the time not to go after them.

But how do we learn which is which? I go by the following steps; my personal Mom-list:

- If we don't fight this battle, will it be detrimental to Jon?

- Will it be detrimental briefly, meaning he may be uncomfortable at first, but get used to it?

- Or will it be detrimental in the long run?

- Is this battle winnable?

- Is it winnable without going to the mat? (We define going to the mat as bringing in outside help such as lawyers or others. The one time in eighth grade when we spoke to our attorney about the bullying/harassment that Jon was going through he gave us the wise counsel about what to do first, and then said he would come to the IEP meeting as a last resort. Because, he explained, once you bring in legal counsel, all doors of communication usually shut tight.)

- Could we win this battle by playing our good-cop-bad-cop routine? Using my husband's bees-and-honey scenario?

- If we fight this battle will we be burning any bridges that we may need to use later? (Perhaps when we need to retreat?)

- Lastly I go by my Mom-meter. If it doesn't feel right to me, I try to fix it. If fixing it doesn't work and it still feels wrong, I fight it, and try not to regret it.

There have been several battles I insisted on fighting that my husband would have let go. But in the end, he has always supported me in the fight. Slowly, over the years, we have learned "when to hold 'em, when to fold 'em." It may be card playing to some, but to us, it's Jon's life.

If the school system's goal is to give my child a free and appropriate education, why do we have battles? Why is there an us vs. them feeling?

"Get off my back! Please!"—understanding rudeness

Is my son's rudeness/curtness due to autism or due to being a teenager?

On the way to school this morning I realize every word out of my son's mouth since the moment he has gotten out of bed has been laced in rudeness. "Whatever!" "Yessss." "Don't talk to me." "Shhhhh…" I get fed up and point this out to him ending with the admonishment, "So, lose the attitude, okay?"

"Yes, yes." He says in a less surly voice.

After I drop him at the front door, asking him to please be polite to people today, the above question circles through my head and I decide I probably need to discuss it. Because if this rudeness he carries with him is part of autism, then I'm once again expecting something from him that he may be incapable of doing. (Goodness knows, it wouldn't be the first time.) But if this rudeness is due to teenage attitude, I can reprimand him for it and work really hard at changing it.

I think back through the last ten years or so, Jon is now 16, and try to think when this attitude started. Was my son always rude to others?—Rude, no. Curt, yes. To the point? Always.

One day when he was in about third grade I remember picking him up from school as I was just returning from the beauty shop. He got in, we talked about school that day (which of course is like pulling teeth), and I said, "Jon, look at me. I got my hair done. Do you like it?" I wasn't fishing for a compliment, I was trying to make eye contact with him, and since I had gone from straight hair to curly perm, I wanted him to notice the change. He looked at me for the first time since getting in the car and, reaching over, plastered both hands on the sides of my head. "No!" He yelled. "Fix it! Put it back."

I laughed at this reaction. "You don't like it?"

He kept trying to smooth out the curls. "NO!"

Okay. So much for hairstyles, I thought.

At another time I remember him telling my mom, right after my dad died, "Grandmom, you look sick! Are you dying too?" She had lost 15 pounds after my dad's death. She tried to laugh it off, although I noticed it was more difficult for her. At that time, I explained to Jon that he has to be careful and not always say what he is thinking.

"Why?" He wanted to know.

"Well, because you may hurt someone's feelings. Or they may think you are being rude or hateful." He nodded his head.

Fast forward to sixth grade. His teacher sends a note home that Jon has been rude to her and the other teacher that day. Telling them when they try to help him, "Go away! I got it! I got it!" She says they are working with him on speaking to others in a polite manner. Once again, when he gets home I remind him that he has to say things differently. "You can't tell people, especially teachers, 'Go away!' They are trying to help you."

"But I didn't need their help," he says.

"Well, you could tell them, 'No thanks, I got it,' so they don't think you are being rude."

"Ohhhh, okay…I didn't know that," he says.

Eighth grade this time. A note comes home telling us he is telling his aide, "Leave me alone."

"You can't be telling teachers to leave you alone," I explain. "You need to learn to be polite when talking to teachers. Say, I'm fine. I'm okay. I don't need help right now, thank you."

He just looks at me.

"Would you want someone to tell you, 'Leave me alone'?"

He shrugs his shoulders. "I didn't need her to help me."

"But you can't be rude about it," I say, adding the alternate phrases he needs to say to adults and teachers.

"Whatever," he says, with another shrug.

At this same time, I am talking to Emily Perl Kingsley, the author of the poem *Welcome to Holland*. I called to get permission to use the poem in my first book, *Parent to Parent*, and we ended up chatting like old friends. She asks me about my son, I ask about hers.

I comment that at that moment, Jon is going through a rude phase and I am wondering if this is autism or teenage or both. She tells me when her son got to High School he was constantly telling people, herself included, "Get off my back!"

We laugh about this, comparing it to Jon's "Leave me alone!" She says she finally did get her son to say, "Get off my back! Please!" We laugh again.

That was eighth grade, we are a year further down the road, High School. Have his manners improved? Have I figured out if this is autism-related or teenage-driven?

Once again, I was able to listen to an expert on this. When Dr. Temple Grandin was interviewed on National Public Radio's *All Things Considered*, the main topic was her book, *Animals in Translation*, and during the interview she stated that she wrote this book to try to explain how and why animals communicate the way they do. A lot of it she related to autistic behavior because she believes there are so many similarities between the two.

As always, every time I listen to Dr. Grandin, I learn something eye-opening about my son. At one point during this interview she talked about using the frontal lobe of the brain to process things and how autistics and animals don't have much frontal lobe going on. She also said that there is a natural filtering system in more advanced brain and frontal lobe function and this is another thing that autistics and animals don't do. They don't filter, they react; animals with so-called animal instinct, and autistics by saying the first thing that pops into their head. No filtering or advance frontal lobe function going on at all.

Ah ha!

This is why Jon and Emily's son display what we consider rude behavior. They want to be "left alone" or they want others to "get off their back" so they naturally say so. They don't have any filtering system going on.

Another Ah ha!

Perhaps the reason this behavior started cropping up in Junior High and High School is because this is the time when teenager, adolescent-type attitudes also appear? The non-filtering is the autism, but the words are part of the typical teenage attitude. Jon tells people to leave him alone. A neurotypical teen may feel the same way, but they have a filtering system, and know not to say it.

It was like a light went on inside my head, and I realized that this too goes back to the fact that Jon lacks common sense. You know, the sense we all develop over the years that tells us if we spit into the wind it will come back and slap us in the face.

I was reminded of this lack of common sense during our Christmas trip to Hawaii. We were on an island bus tour and had stopped at one of the North Shore beaches for 15 minutes of watching the surfers and the ten-foot-high waves. The bus driver had warned us that if we played too close to the water, we may get surprised and get drenched, and then we would be wet the rest of the ride.

I took this warning to heart, and when I took my sandals off to play, and Jon took his shoes off, I constantly warned him to get back, as each wave seemed to grow larger and closer. My husband stood back and took pictures and told me, "Let him go, he is having fun."

You guessed it, fun stopped when a large wave hit him up to the knees of his shorts and soaked a tennis shoe and a sock that was sitting in the sand. We trudged back to the bus. He was wet. He was upset. He was on the verge of meltdown. We climbed onto the bus and tried to sit as quietly as possible in our seats without disturbing the other passengers.

I moved to sit next to him, and for the next 20 minutes or so I coached him in a quiet voice to calm down, he was okay. He should have listened to my warnings, this was his choice that he made, and now he knew the consequences of his choice. As he tried to keep from crying and melting down totally, I worked at trying to dry him off and brush the sand away.

At one point he said, "Mom, you should have pulled me out of there, kicking and screaming."

"No," I told him quietly. "You are 15 now. You need to learn to make your own choices and live with the outcome."

We spoke quietly until we got to the next stop and by the time we were touring the Dole Pineapple Plantation, he was actually *almost* okay. I was very, very proud of him.

Later on when I look at the pictures my husband took of him on the beach I see a tall gangly youth in shorts, running with abandon at the waves, having the time of his life. We don't have pictures from the aftermath of the wave. But I will never forget the hard lesson he learned in common sense and consequences, and I'm sure he won't forget it either. This is how Jon develops any filtering or frontal lobe function, only through experiences, which then go into his memory bank or onto his hard drive.

Thus, relating this to manners and being rude, he doesn't have the filtering ability to sugar-coat his feelings, so, this too, he has to learn verbatim. Not only does he have to learn manners like other kids do, he has to learn the words that go with the manners.

Emily's son finally learned to tell others, "Get off my back! Please!" Jon has told teachers, "Leave me alone! Please!"

Some teachers realize this is good for him, that this may be all that he can verbalize at the moment. Other teachers send notes home about his rudeness, at which time he and I go through alternate phrases for him to say, again.

Me? I'm just thankful my question is answered. His curtness is the autism—he can't come up with the right words to express his feelings. His rudeness is teenage attitude, as in typical "leave me alone, whatever, shrug of the shoulders" attitude. The curtness I will gladly help him try to overcome. The rudeness? No Gameboy for the weekend, no TV for the night, normal punishments for normal attitude problems. Works for me.

If my son has always been about two years behind socially, compared to neuro-typical kids, does this mean he will go through this teenage phase two years longer than others?

Chapter Thirteen

An interview with a parent expert—Emily Perl Kingsley

What are your hopes?

When considering who to interview for this very important chapter, I wanted to get the thoughts of someone who had been *there*—"the land of disability"—longer than I have. Someone who has weathered the storms and has lived to tell about it. I immediately thought of Emily. Not only is she an Emmy-award-winning writer for television including *Sesame Street*, but she has been her son Jason's advocate (who has Down Syndrome) going on 30-odd years. I explained to her the basic question was "What are your hopes?" and we went from there.

Me: Your son is now a young man and you have been living and working with him, and this disability for a time now. Looking back, how would you hope things have changed for other parents who are now going through what you went through?

Emily: In our day, the belief was that people with Down Syndrome were all "moderately-to-severely retarded" and were not routinely given the opportunity to learn academics. We had to fight hard to get people to accept the fact that our son was beginning to read and had academic skills that entitled him to an education. In those days, kids with DS were taught "life skills" and not much else. Nowadays it is accepted that kids with DS will read and write and do math. They are also included in the ordinary activities of school to a much greater degree that we had. Because of these improvements, new parents get a much brighter outlook when the baby is first born. Outreach programs are in place to counsel and support new families and give them accurate and current information as well as referrals to early intervention programs. With this support, families get off to a much better start—which bodes well for the child's development and the comfort of the entire family.

Me: If you had the ear of an important government official how would you hope to change things affecting your son's life?

Emily: It is essential that children with special needs receive the education and supports they need in order to maximize their potential and help them develop into productive contributing citizens. In this way, they are able to participate in the community and not be a drain on public resources. Cutting funds to special education is a particularly short-sighted and self-defeating policy. It is in everyone's best interest to make people with disabilities as capable and productive as possible.

Me: What do you hope for at this present moment for your son?

Emily: My son is working part-time at a radio station. I would love for the job to be expanded so he would have more time on the job and more income. In addition, this job is in a remote location and public transportation is not convenient. I hope to be able to arrange some better way of getting him to and from the job…or get him a job he would enjoy in a better location.

Me: What would you hope for his daily life? Or short-term goals and hopes?

Emily: He is working on skills in his group home—three young men in a private home with part-time supervision. I hope he will improve his cooking and awareness of nutrition and healthy eating habits. I also hope he will do more socializing—reaching out and contacting friends, making dates and taking over more responsibility for his recreation life.

Me: What should parents out there hope for with their children or young adults who carry a disability?

Emily: The most important goal is to realize a lifestyle which accommodates the disability but allows for dignity, productivity, and personal happiness. People with disabilities have all the same hopes, dreams, goals, and feelings as other people—which should be recognized and acknowledged. But it's also important to realize that people with disabilities are *individuals*—with their own ideas, opinions, and tastes. This must also be taken into account when setting up living situations, jobs, and relationships. Parents should hope that their children will be included and accepted by their community, have friends, jobs, and a full life to the maximum extent possible.

Me: Have you ever found yourself in a seemingly hopeless situation with your son?

Emily: My son became depressed after the death of my husband—his father. He became angry and oppositional. It was extremely difficult and frustrating. He began psychotherapy, which was helpful but did not completely resolve the situation. He also was on various antidepressant medications.

Recently we did a wide battery of tests and discovered that he has a rather severe case of sleep apnea—which, I found out, occurs in 60 percent of individuals with Down Syndrome. He is sleep deprived and, as a result, is tired, and that contributed to his irritability.

He is now using a continuous positive airway pressure (CPAP) machine plus a mild antidepressant, is continuing with his psychotherapy—and we see marked improvement in his mood and his general demeanor. He is taking better care of himself—grooming and hygiene—s performing better at work and with friends, and is enjoying life much more.

People with Down Syndrome can benefit from psychotherapy just like anybody else. It's sometimes hard to find a therapist who has expertise with this population, but it can be very helpful. Our kids have so many challenges in their lives and often have a diminished ability to articulate their problems and fewer professionals to go to for help. We have an obligation to seek out whatever help they need in meeting the challenges that go along with living with a disability in this complicated world.

Me: On a more personal note, where do you get your hope? What keeps you from running screaming into the night? How do you keep hope?

Emily: There are definitely times I want to crawl back into bed, pull the covers up and say, "Who asked for this??!?!" And I believe that you need to do that once in a while, just to preserve your sanity. But it's still your child, and any improvement you see gives you fresh energy to carry on.

The biggest obstacles have not come from my child—but rather from fighting ignorance and bigotry, inadequate programs and insensitive people. This child is as entitled to a full happy life as any other child I might have had, and while the rewards may be different, they can be great and fulfilling. It's important not to dwell on *what he might have been*, but rather on *what he is*.

Me: Do you have specific hopes for your family at this time?

Emily: I am hoping to take Jason for a vacation—just the two of us—some time soon. We haven't been away together for some time, and we always enjoy the trips we take together.

Me: What do you hope for in your son's future?

Emily: I hope he will find a job that he truly loves, which utilizes his abilities and gives him personal gratification. I hope he will gain some peace within himself. He is angry about the fact that he was born with a disability and is very much aware of how he was "short changed" in life. He is bitter and resentful of the fact that there are so many dreams and goals which he will never be able to realize. I hope he will come to some kind of reconciliation which will allow him to enjoy his life more fully.

I hope he will expand his circle of friends and possibly form a romantic loving attachment for his future. I think he wants this very much, but the opportunities to explore romantic relationships have been very limited. He has the same goals of marriage, sexuality, family and permanence as anyone else—and I hope, to the best of his ability, that he will be able to realize these dreams.

Me: How would you hope things would change, in the world, when it comes to your son and how they—all of the theys out there—deal with him?

Emily: I would hope that the disability rights movement makes the kind of permanent changes that former rights movements—women's rights, civil rights, etc.—have accomplished. So many people with disabilities are prejudged based on external appearances, negative stereotypes, and archaic misinformation. We still have a long way to go until the general population is more understanding and accepting of people with individual differences.

People need to be seen as *individuals* with their own unique abilities, ideas, opinions, and personalities. Improvement has been made but not nearly enough. Yet.

Me: What would be your final word to other parents regarding disability and hope? Do you feel that the two don't go together?

Emily: Keep fighting for what your child is entitled to. It's not an optimal situation, but it can be managed. Remember to acknowledge the pain of the loss of your original dream. This is not the best thing that ever happened to you! But having acknowledged that, you can go on and make the best life for yourself and your child that you can.

Me: Have you ever asked your son what his hopes are?

Emily: Often his hopes are unrealistic. He wants to direct animated films for the Disney Corporation. He is just waiting for his big break! He wants to be married, have a family, and live entirely independently. I do not promise him anything, but tell him to keep working towards his goals.

I do tell him that directing films for the Disney Corporation is an unrealistic goal. He is not trained to do that. He sometimes talks about wanting to become a doctor. I ask him if he really wants to go back to school—four years of college, four years of medical school, residency, etc., etc.—and he ultimately realizes that it's a bit of a stretch.

But I'm glad that he has dreams and goals. He has accomplished great things already—his book, *Count Us In: Growing Up with Down Syndrome* is still selling very well and is planned for a Spanish language translation soon. He continues to contribute articles and chapters for books and has been invited to join a New York State Self Advocacy Speakers' Bureau to give presentations on self-determination.

It's very tough to balance the elaborate dreams with the sometimes harsh realities and keep his self-esteem intact! That's the hardest balancing act I have right now. To keep his goals realistic and within reach without diminishing his ego—it's a real challenge!

But he's my kid and I love him and somehow, together, we'll get through this life and make the most of it we can!!

Does anyone else notice, it doesn't matter what the disability, a parent's hope for their disabled child is very similar, right down to the goals?

Stopping to note success—
a trip to the dentist

Life gets so hectic that sometimes I have to force myself to stop and take stock of things. Where we were; how far we've come. Not necessarily where we are going, I think on that too much.

This past week was Jon's monthly orthodontist appointment. He always stresses about these monthly appointments, even if they usually only last about 30 minutes. Just long enough for the Doc to change his rubber-bands. On the way in the car, while he is stressing, I try to remind him that he has done this before.

"You have never gone there and died?"

"No."

"You have always lived through this experience?"

"Yes. But the pain…and then I can't eat."

"You have always been able to eat dinner the night after the appointment. It's just a little sore."

"Yeah…"

"You have never starved to death after your appointments."

He laughs. "Nope."

"Okay. So I think today you can do this without crying, don't you?"

"I don't cry because of the pain. I cry when it's all over because it worries me."

"Okay. But you are 15, not a baby. I think you can do this now without crying don't you?"

He actually scratches his chin as if he is contemplating this suggestion, and slowly nods his head.

We arrive, he freaks out as usual over the dentist office smells. We have a different technician this time, although we've asked to have the same one every time. It's a little rough-going at first, but he calms down and waits for the Doc to come in and put the rubber-bands back on that the technician has taken off.

This doctor has the best bedside manner of any dentist or orthodontist I have ever known. He is the best with Jon. Jon asks him several questions about the way his teeth are moving and looking. He smiles and takes time to answer them.

While Jon is trying to handle the pressure of getting the new bands on, I talk, trying to distract him.

"You know, I was just thinking that in one more month it will be our anniversary. We've been coming a year in January."

"I expect flowers, Jon," I hear the Doc say. He finishes quickly and scoots his chair back.

Now to look in the mirror. Jon jumps up after every visit to see the results in the mirror.

"I remember the routine now," Doc says.

And surprisingly, we are out of there, no tears this time!

On the way home I congratulate Jon on this major accomplishment and remind him that I knew he could do this.

"Okay, so can I get a reward?" he slyly asks.

I laugh. "You are eating your reward." We had just gone through a drive-through for burger and fries.

"Okay," he concedes.

The next day, on my way to work I think about successes. What an amazing feat this has become, these braces. Just getting Jon, with tactile problems, to sit in the chair a year ago and stand for them to make a mold of his teeth was something. And then to tolerate the pressure in his mouth every month as wires and bands are changed and tightened. I shake my head in wonder as I think about it. My autistic son has done something amazing and at times I am stunned by it. I was the last of four children in my family, the only one who didn't get braces back then. They were either out of money by the time they got to me, or too busy. (Probably both.) So I can't even imagine what my son is going through.

Thoreau writes in his conclusion to *On Walden Pond*, "If one advances confidently in the direction of his dreams, and endeavors to live the life which he has imagined, he will meet with a success unexpected in the common hours." Jon doesn't realize this, but he has "met with a success unexpected in the common hours." There were no loud hurrahs, no fireworks—just success.

I may have been the one to advance confidently and it may have been my dream imagined, but it was Jon's success! I'm glad I stopped to take note.

Chapter Fourteen

Planning for our own demise

An interview with an attorney

Remember: it is not given to man to take his goods with
him...

(Tomb of Egyptian king Inyotef 2600 BC)

How can we live out our lives peacefully?

A year or so ago my husband twisted my arm and talked me into finding
an attorney to write a will. We had already talked *about* a will. Having
taken several plane trips as a family and as a couple, we had always
discussed "what if" and had made calls to family members with instructions on if something would happen to both of us. But this time...this
time he was serious. Although the thoughts of our death depressed me, I
let him talk me into it.

We found ourselves talking with Donald W. Ingrum, a local attorney.
Going into the meeting, we thought everything was pretty cut and dried.
Coming out, we realized that this wasn't so, and we were very thankful
we had found an experienced attorney. At the very beginning of our
introductions and preliminary questions, Don learned that we had a son
who had a disability, and we learned that having a child with a disability
takes a little more planning than we had thought. We ended up setting
up a living trust, with Jon as the beneficiary. Yes, it sounds simple on
paper, but it wasn't.

So when I started thinking about what other parents ought to do, my
thoughts turned to my least favorite topic—planning for our own
demise. I went back and asked Don this question and a few more. Don
speaks in the context of the legal system in the state of Missouri, but

similar legal provisions are likely to apply in other common law jurisdictions in the US, the UK, and elsewhere. So, wherever you are, you can use what Don says as a general guide, but please seek legal advice locally before making any decisions.

Me: What ought a parent do in planning for the future when they have a child with a disability?

Don: I have a questionnaire that I hand out to parents when they come in. It asks about family members, and those questions it asks are about ages, not only parents, but children, and so on. Another one of the questions I have is: Do you have any children with disabilities or anybody with special needs? Whether it's a disability or maybe it's somebody who is a spendthrift, maybe they are normal otherwise, but they just don't handle money very well, or maybe really badly.

Usually this question is one of the things that brings it to the parents' attention, where they then realize they ought to do something. Frequently I find that people do their own planning and they say, well, I'll leave everything to my other children, with the idea that that child will take care of the child with the disability. When that's really not a very good way to handle the situation. Number one, the child you may leave the money to, to take care of this disabled child, may have creditor problems, marital problems, or dies. Lots of things could happen that you don't anticipate and often times this could leave the child with the disability out there adrift, without anybody to protect him or her.

One of the things I encourage people to do if they have a child with disabilities, depending on what their financial circumstances are, how many other children there are, what their objectives are, is to try to make the most efficient use of whatever money they do have. Whether they want to leave the whole amount of money or just a portion of it, they need to try to set it up carefully, because there are a number of government programs available, and at least from my perspective, the last thing you want to do is to have this child lose eligibility for those government programs because of the way things are structured.

There are various ways of doing that. There's the Missouri Family Trust; this is where you can leave money to this trust and set up a separate account for them. The money that is in that trust is used for extras, it doesn't disqualify them for any government programs. The downside of this is after the disabled child is gone, whatever is remaining goes to the

Missouri Family Trust, which is a self-perpetuating fund. Typically this is what I do for people who have something that they want to put in place for the disabled child for after their deaths, or it could be siblings who set something up for this child, I set it up into a trust so that the money can be used for their benefit to provide extras rather than to replace the government programs that exist. That's generally what I do. The other side of it, besides just the monetary part of it, is making some sort of provision depending on the extent of the disability of the child or the person, is asking: Who is going to be the guardian, who are they going to live with? What sort of arrangements does the family want to make in that respect?

Me: I know there is a difference between estates, trusts, and wills. Suppose a family comes in and they say: we have a will, we've named this child in our will, and that's what we are going to do. Why should there be a difference between a trust and will for this child? Is there a difference in this case?

Don: There is. You can create a trust within the will itself. For instance, I can own property, and we have a disabled child. Maybe we have it set up so that if something happens to one of us the other automatically gets everything, upon the death of the survivor of the two of us, a trust is created. Then at that time, whatever the provisions for that child are in the trust, those things are effective. What you do not want to happen is to say: everything to each other and then after we're gone, if you have three children, it's split into three shares equally. When that happens if a share goes to a disabled child, two things will happen. Number one, if the disability is severe enough, then a conservator will be appointed by the probate court to look after the money, and two, it will probably disqualify that child from any governmental benefits, whether Medicaid or whatever it might be. Those are the things that you don't want to do.

You can set up a living trust where you transfer assets into a trust currently, and then maybe this child's share will continue on in a trust, whereas the share to the other children may be distributed outright to them upon your death. Or you could set up one big trust, leave everything in a trust and leave it up to the trustee on how the money is to be spent for maybe the disabled and the non-disabled children or child.

Me: What's the least a parent should do? Suppose they feel they have no inheritable assets? They are working nine to five, have car payments, don't own property?

Don: What I would do is use the Missouri Family Trust. They could put money into this trust and whether you put it in currently or at your death, it is in a segregated account, and used to supplement the governmental programs in place for your child so there will be extras for them. I suspect each state will have a similar program because it's Medicaid driven. What it is intended to do is to allow families to leave money to disabled children and make funds available to them without disqualifying them for governmental or Medicaid benefits. So I would just about guarantee there is something like this in every state.

Me: So the main thing the parent needs to look at is not only assets but benefits. They don't want their assets to affect the child's benefits after they are gone?

Don: I encourage parents to do that, because to me if there are government benefits in place and if you want to set things up so that you can provide extras for that child, then to me, that's what the parent's money is for. To enhance the quality of life.

Me: Another thing that will affect my husband and me, and many parents out there, is what do we do when our child turns 18? Do we apply for continued guardianship? How does a parent go about that? When?

Don: What I generally suggest to people is that prior to the child actually reaching 18 years of age, maybe shortly before, that you come in and talk about that. If a guardianship is appropriate, then we go from there. The thing in Missouri is that you need to distinguish between guardianships and conservatorships. Guardianships have to do with the type of care the person is going to receive. Conservatorships deal with who takes care of the money. A lot of the other states still use Guardian of the Person and Guardian of the Estate, but it has been changed in Missouri.

Where I think it's important to give some considerations to the guardianship when the child turns 18 is you can run into potential problems in terms of medical care or consent for medical care. Before a person reaches age 18, under the law you have the right to give consent to medical treatment, you have the right to decide where he is going to go to school. But once the child reaches age 18, absent of some sort of finding of incapacity or disability, then he is an adult. So there has to be some sort of court action to say, hey, there is a situation here where the child should not have total control over the decisions he makes, and there needs to be a guardianship or conservatorship established, or both.

Then you get to the issue, until about 15–20 years ago in Missouri, you were either totally disabled and incapacitated or you weren't. You were either functioning or you were non-functioning. It's no longer that way, and in fact, probably, and myself included, frequently, when somebody comes in and has a child who is disabled, they will say, we need to have this guardianship established, for medical purposes, etc.... Frequently, the child has no separate money of his or her own. Basically it's what they get from the parents or, if they work, the sheltered workshop or wherever it might be. We go in and we say the child is disabled and needs a guardian appointed, and bingo, that's it.

Now in Missouri, and probably several states, I became aware that Missouri has a provision that you can have a *limited* guardianship or a *limited* conservatorship, so that it's tailor-made to that individual's abilities, and what their needs are. For example I've set one up for a young man who although he had court-appointed conservators controlling his money, the money he earned from working, there was a special provision that he was allowed to maintain this money in a checking account of his own. He was allowed to write checks on the account. There was a pre-printed statement on the check, "Not good for amounts over $200.00." So if he wanted to go to the store and buy something, he could do so. We even had a provision that limited not only individual checks but that he could not enter into any contracts in the amount of x dollars. I think in the last 20 years, most states have allowed limited guardianship or limited conservatorship.

Another thing that I just read in the paper was that there is a provision in the Missouri constitution and there is a statute enacted pursuant to it, that if you are under a guardianship you are not allowed to vote in the state of Missouri. What brought it to a head was there was a former law professor from the University of Illinois who was a schizophrenic. The thrust of the suit was that despite being under a guardianship, he was probably much more capable of understanding some of the issues in regards to choosing our national leaders than a lot of other people who are allowed to vote. So there was a suit filed in the Federal Court in Kansas City to allow him to vote in the elections.

This brought to my way of thinking that if you can tailor-make your guardianship to take care of situations like he can write checks up to *x* dollars, there should be no reason that we shouldn't be able to tailor-make the guardianship that if you have somebody who has the capability of voting, then we shouldn't deny them that right either.

These are the sort of things that I think as people become more sensitive and more aware of the options that are available, they will be used more. Now if you go in and you want a *cookie-cutter guardianship* then you are not going to get the right to vote, you are not going to get the right to write checks on an account that you own personally.

Me: Most of our kids are going from learning to be as independent as possible in High School, hopefully going to college or a job and then at the age of 18, we don't want to stymie them. Limited guardianship could be exactly what we want to try to help them continue to succeed.

Don: Yes, to try to get them to live to their maximum potential. I suspect, although I don't know for a fact, but I'm not sure if this limited guardianship/conservatorship was directed so much at young people who have disabilities as it was maybe directed at older people who were starting to lose some of their function, but again at the same time shouldn't be denied all of their rights. It has helped people on both ends of the spectrum [*Author's note:* life spectrum in this case, not autism spectrum]. And at least the vehicle is there to tailor-make it to the individual situation so that we take away as few rights as possible while at the same time allowing them to live as normal a life as possible.

Me: If there is a limited guardianship set up, and perhaps this child gets married later in life, late twenties, thirties, does this guardianship need to be changed? How does marriage affect this?

Don: In terms of having somebody who is under guardianship and they do get married, I would say, number one, the guardianship would have to consent to the marriage. In all likelihood this would be something that the person could not do on his own. He wouldn't have the legal capacity to enter into a marriage contract. But assuming that the marriage took place with authority, then at that point, depending on who the person married, if it was somebody else who was under a disability, it stands to reason that the spouse is not going to become the guardian. If it is somebody who is not under a disability then the guardianship would continue, but with a different guardian.

Me: If a parent has a disabled child, can any attorney help them?

Don: I think most attorneys do guardianship work. Some don't. As far as doing a guardianship if you do a *cookie-cutter guardianship* then just about anybody can do that. If you want to tailor-make it to the young adult's situation then you may want to have somebody who has had more experience dealing with it. Probably where it becomes more important to have somebody who has done this type of work is when you start dealing with money. I'm not saying everything is money driven, but you don't want to wind up with a situation where funds are dissipated that don't need to be dissipated.

Me: So parents need to ask questions, they need to interview attorneys?

Don: I think they need to find out if they have had some experience in the Medicaid area and the planning area. And also you don't want to, say, disqualify a young person from voting if they have the ability to do that. I think it's doing a disservice to them. So if someone says, you can't do that, well, that's not true. If you can convince the judge that the person is capable of doing this, then the law is set up so that you can do it. You can let that person have the ability to vote, or to drive, if they are capable of doing it.

Me: What is the worst-case scenario that could happen if we hadn't come in and set up a trust to take care of Jon?

Don: Probably what would have happened, say, if you had done nothing and you both got run over by a truck, and Jon was left, whatever funds you had would have gone to Jon, he would have been sole owner of those funds. There would be a court-appointed guardian for him and I would say even at the age he is now, he would probably be disqualified from receiving any programs that are "need based." So with the money that you guys left to him, depending on the level of care that was needed and what needed to be done, he would have had to pay his own way. In terms of the downside to him, it's kind of a two-edged sword. On the one hand the money is under court supervision, which is not necessarily all bad because you have someone watching the person who is taking care of the money, making sure annual settlements are filed, and making sure there are not any investments made that are risky investments. But not risky doesn't necessarily mean prudent because for someone at his age with a normal life expectancy if you are investing in nothing but fixed income securities, that money is probably not going to last for his lifetime, and any money will be eaten up. The advantage of utilizing a trust is you have more flexibility as far as investments, and it's not as costly to maintain as a court-appointed guardianship or conservatorship.

Me: What's the most important thing you wish to tell a reader of this book if they have a child who has a disability diagnosis? Of course, first of all they are trying to handle that diagnosis, and the school system, but what is the other thing, most important to you, that they should be doing?

Don: I think the thing that strikes me the most, and what so many parents worry about, is what's going to happen when I'm no longer here? I'm not talking about just financially, I'm talking about where the child is going to live, how they are going to live. Who is going to be looking after them to make sure they are okay? Not that there is anything wrong with public agencies or public administrators offices, but when you have two or three hundred clients that you are responsible for, it's just impossible for the public administrator or any other governmental employee to really look after the clients the way they should. If I were a parent with a disabled child, the thing that I would want to do is to try to, number one, make the maximum use of my resources if something would happen to me, and then, number two, try to have some sort of plan in place so that you've designated in advance not only who's going to look after the money but who's going to kind of be there for the child, or the adult at this point.

Me: And this should all be done in writing?

Don: Oh, yes. I wouldn't place much confidence in informal relation-ships. And the reason I say that is I think that putting it down in writing makes you think about not only who you might want to use, but what happens if something happens to those people? Oftentimes you are not talking about a two- or three-year period, but several decades. I think what it forces the parents of the disabled person to do is to think, okay, if something happens to me and I have so and so as the one who is respon-sible for this child, this person might not be around further down the road. If all of these people fail or are gone, then the court will have to appoint someone, and hopefully there will be some other family member able to step up and fill that void.

I thanked Don for trying to teach me "everything I needed to know but was afraid to ask" in planning for the future for my son, and I came away with several thoughts.

- A plan must be made for a disabled child, even if it is only the realization that because you are not setting up a trust or putting a plan in writing, if something should happen to you, the state will take over the care of your child. Even not making a plan, after reading this chapter, has become your plan.

- In setting up a trust, do shop around and find an attorney who has worked with Medicaid and guardianship/conservatorship issues. Why not find someone with the best knowledge out there?

- A limited guardianship/conservatorship at the age of 18 is not such a scary beast. Once you think about it, it really is just a continuation of the IEP you wrote and implemented for you child every year he/she was in school. And who is the best expert to set this up? You and your attorney of course.

- Setting up a living trust for Jon is to enhance his life and give him the extras he may need to live his life, not to make him ineligible for the services he is entitled to. A careful attorney needs to watch for this.

- Putting in writing that my sister or my husband's brother will be guardian in case something should happen to both of us may not be enough. It's time to talk to my son's older cousins and find the right one to do the job if necessary. This too needs to be in writing.

- Planning for my own death may be depressing, but so have been many things in my life such as the first IEP meeting I ever attended and several meetings thereafter.

Alas, as I left our attorney's office, I found myself crying on the way home. Was I depressed? Maybe. It has never been one of my favorite topics of conversation, death and dying and estate planning. But I think the tears could only be described as typical of parents of a child with a disability. Once again, every aspect of our life is affected by this diagnosis, right down to planning for our own demise. This meeting with Don brought it home in every intimate detail, that Jon is *not* normal, he has a disability. And I can't let my guard down a minute, not even in death.

Sometimes even when I do what I ought to do, peace doesn't come. How normal is this?

chicken nugget #14

Changing my view

Today I got up and sometime during my regular morning routine I realized what I need at this moment is a different perspective, or according to *Rodale's Synonym Finder*, a different view, viewpoint or mental outlook. Yes, *mental outlook* is what I'm looking for.

Jon has started High School. He is in his second full week and already I've been dealing with his stress, my stress, and quite a bit of confusion with his teachers, the new aide, and his new caseworker. I know it will probably all work out, but right now it is a little rough on everyone. I hate it when he is stressed. I hate it when he feels confused. I hate it when he feels like the weight of the world is on his shoulders. I've already been angry with the school on two occasions and have realized that I certainly am acting like a "parent from hell" which I try to avoid.

So while all of these thoughts are swirling round and round in my head, I suddenly realize that maybe I need a new perspective on the situation. I sit a few moments, trying to take a break from the morning rush and whirl of thoughts, and I wonder, "How does one acquire a new perspective or develop a new mental outlook."

One way, which always worked for me in the past, has been to focus on the positive. Yes, Jon is having difficulty adjusting to High School and his teachers adjusting to him, but it could be worse. Lord knows I cling to the fact that at most times Jon is high-functioning. Yes, right now he is more autistic than not, because of the new environment he is in, and because he must learn to communicate with new people—both of these feats have always been difficult for him. So right now, at this moment in time, he is displaying the most autistic-like behaviors he has ever displayed.

But isn't the first month or so of school always like that for him? If I force myself to think back or go so far as to read least year's journal at about this same time, I will probably see that the beginning of eighth grade was just as difficult for him, just as stressful for me. And didn't things calm down? Well, actually eighth grade turned out to be the year from hell, but this was because of a bullying problem we had. But yes, honestly, if it hadn't been for the bullying issue, eighth grade would have calmed down and been okay.

So too, this year should begin to flow. He should be able to soon feel comfortable at his new school, comfortable with his new teachers and they with him. Things will get better…

Another thing that works for me is knowledge. If I am confused about something, I look it up and read about it. Wondering, am I doing the right thing with Jon in a particular situation? I research the topic to death. Stressing about an issue? Find an expert, or someone else out there who has been there before me, to calm my fears.

So in this case, I get on the internet for about a day and do a search under topics such as autism and High School, or teaching high-functioning autistic students and High School. I am pleased to find a lot out there; some I've read before, such as a web article by Dr. Temple Grandin titled *Choosing the Right Job for People with Autism or Asperger's Syndrome* (Grandin 1999). This article deals more with finding jobs for later in life, but also has information on what to do while the student is still in High School. I also find a wonderful, short and concise paper by Leslie S. Klein, PhD titled *Asperger's Students in High School* (2002). I read through this one, underlining what applies to Jon and plan to make copies to take to our first IEP meeting.

I find a PowerPoint project geared towards educators by Sheila Wagner of the Emory Autism Center in Atlanta, titled *Middle School Madness and High School Hysterics*. I laugh at the title as I print the slides down and then read them. After going through the advice given for Middle School, I come to the slide for High School which states: "But what about High School? *We are flat running out of time!*" (Wagner 2004, p.12). Oh no, I think, this is exactly how I feel! Is it too late to help my son?

After reading through the rest of her slides and her very practical advice I calm down a little and begin to make my own list:

- Goals for graduation need to be aiming for lifetime goals. He needs to graduate with a job, some type of job, whether he will be going on to college or not.

- And what about college? Vocational Technical School, a typical four-year college, or Junior College?

- He should have a goal to make friends while in High School.

- We must encourage him to join a club at school.

- We need to eliminate problem behaviors before he gets into the real world. Teach him to use a Palm Pilot. He is so into computers and technical things, he will probably love it.

- We need to try to teach to his interests, or he won't perform, care, or even try.

I make this list and come to Wagner's last slide, which reads, "Creating a Vision—Depends on You. What will happen if you don't have a vision for your students [read children]?" (p.37). Thus, after two days of working on changing my perspective, acquiring a new mental outlook, I feel 100 percent better about High School. I can now focus on positive behavior, events, and issues with Jon, and once again, I have a plan. I have a new list for High School and I have some wonderful information to take to our upcoming IEP meeting. Instead of thoughts of frustration, anger, and depression swirling around in my head, I now feel positive, strong, and back in control.

Every change is a challenge for Jon. We knew that High School would be a big one. But it will not sink him; this challenge is *do-able*, just as all of the other challenges in his life up to this point have been. And because I have changed my perspective I can now help my son change his. Because I have calmed my stress and my fears, I can now calm his. Isn't a new perspective great!

Now I can go and change the perspective of all of his teachers, in a calm, friendly way—of course!

Chapter Fifteen
Resources Remix
Useful information and resources

I only ask for information.

(Charles Dickens 1850)

Where is the best place to go for information?

What an information age we live in. Anyone can sit down at the computer, type in literally any word, and come up with a million sites where that one word is mentioned.

Unfortunately, this wealth of information also leads to a wealth of confusion. In this chapter, I only want to tell you about resources which I have personally looked at or used, or organizations that I belong to. If you want to see the million hits on autism, feel free to do so, but that may not help you find the information you need without a long drawn-out search.

Thus, listed here are organizations that I have belonged to, and sources that are, at this moment in time, up and running, and available. As always, feel free to pick and choose and use what meets your needs.

Organizations

The Autism Society of America (www.autism-society.org).
I have belonged to the ASA since Jon was first diagnosed almost ten years ago. You can't find a better organization to help you stay current in all aspects of this disability. They know how to be cautious, they know how to help parents, and they know how to give us the information we need

to know before we may even realize we need it. Local ASA chapters can also be found. Unfortunately there has never been one in our area.

MAAP Services, Inc. (maapservices.org).
This organization which began simply as MAAP, now extends their name as services for More advanced individuals with Autism, Asperger's syndrome, and Pervasive developmental disorder (PDD). I have also belonged to this group for going on ten years, and have received their newsletter during that time. Here you will find letters sent by parents and individuals on the spectrum who are trying to connect with others. Susan Moreno may have been the first to remind us that we are not alone in our struggle with this disability, but because of her efforts and this organization, she will not be the last. I have attended several conferences of this community, and although its members are spread all over the world, we are family.

Autism, Asperger Resource Center (www.autismAsperger.org).
This is a local organization in Kansas City that I've belonged to for a few years. They hold very informative, educational conferences, and have useful links on their website.

Websites
The following are websites that I visit regularly and have found to be very helpful.

Online Asperger Syndrome Information and Support (www.udel.edu/bkirby/Asperger/)
This is a wonderful site sponsored by the University of Delaware and posted for parents and educators. If you only visit one site, this one, you will find links for other sites on IEPs, special education law, a bookstore, papers and articles, and much more. This site I visit often to see what is new.

Wrightslaw (www.wrightslaw.com/)
This is where you should go to find out about your rights as parents of a child with a disability. This site will perhaps throw you into information overload, but if you are going to be an informed advocate for your child, you really need to spend some time here. If you are patient, you can go as

deep into this site as you wish and find specific answers to your questions. A parent asked me the other day why my son had an aide, and his did not, when our school districts are in the same state and only an hour away from each other. I suggested he go to Wrightslaw and look into this. I know that when Jon was diagnosed, I was told that for him to be in the regular classroom with an autism diagnosis, he would be given an aide. This was the best placement for him, and it has always been this way. Now that he is in High School, we are trying to work on self-advocacy, and remove the aide while leaving Jon in the classroom. But not being an expert on the law, I could not tell this parent why Jon has an aide and their child doesn't.

The Maze (www.planetautism.com/)
This site, posted by Janet Norman-Bain, I have visited off and on for almost ten years, and I must say, this woman has more energy than I have in a lifetime! She states that her son Alex has autism, and she and her son Ben are on the spectrum. You know you are at her site when the screen turns black and you scroll down through hundreds of links that she has nicely categorized for us. The first time I found her site, I racked up over an hour of online computer time and felt like I had entered another world. Now that I'm more familiar with her constantly growing and *accurate* list of links on autism/Asperger's, I go there, knowing I will be online for a long time and it's worth it. And it is like another world—after all, it is autism.

Books

The World of the Autistic Child, by Bryna Siegel (1996, Oxford University Press).
This book is the resource book that just keeps on giving. I used this book when Jon was younger. I list it here because even though Jon is older, some of the answers are here in this book that I've had on my shelf for almost ten years!

Autism and Learning: A Guide to Good Practice, edited by Stuart Powell and Rita Jordan (1997, David Fulton).
This book was compiled by specialists in the UK. I'm reading this one again as Jon struggles with a difficult science class in High School. At mid-year we had the option of taking him out and putting him into

another more structured, calmer science class, but my husband and I decided that if he can learn to tolerate this setting and this teacher, he will have learned much more than just the subject of science. After looking through it again, I've decided to pass it on to Jon's science teacher so he can read the chapter on teaching science.

Higher Functioning Adolescents and Young Adults with Autism, by Ann Fullerton, Joyce Stratton, Phyllis Coyne and Carol Gray (1996, Pro-Ed). My expensive "teacher's guide." I went back to this one as Jon began High School to look at the chapter on Adapting Instructional Materials and Strategies. High School is all new teachers who didn't have a clue about Jon. Thus we had to start at step one and work our way up with them. This book always helps.

I Openers: Parents Ask Questions About Sexuality and Children with Developmental Disabilities, by Dave Hingsburger (1993, Family Support Institute Press, Canada).
If you've already read my chapter in this book "The s-e-x word meets the a-u-t-i-s-m word," you know why this book is listed here. I know there are other books out there on autism/Asperger's and adolescent issues, but this one is still a keeper.

Asperger Syndrome and Rage, by Brenda Smith Myles and Jack Southwick (1999, Autism Asperger Publications).
We went back to this book during the terrible, horrible, Junior High years when Jon was being bullied and as a result was suspended for punching said bully in the arm.

Right Address ... Wrong Planet: Children with Aspergers Syndrome Becoming Adults, by Gena P. Barnhill (2002, Autism Asperger Publishing).
A book by a wonderful author/professional/mom. After reading this one I was able to "talk" with Gena through e-mail. Her son (and their family) have gone through some difficult times, but her book has great personal insight and information for other parents who are moving into the Asperger's young adult phase of their children's lives. The last time I "spoke" with her, she was working full-time as an autism consultant while still being her son's greatest advocate. I told her then that she was an amazing woman. While I was getting my master's and subbing for the schools, I had to tell the school that although I perhaps had the education and the patience needed, I could not sub in the special services

areas of the schools. My explanation was that I had to live with autism on a daily basis with my son, and I couldn't work with it too. But Gena does, and I tip my hat to her!

Freaks, Geeks and Asperger Syndrome: A User Guide to Adolescence, by Luke Jackson (2002, Jessica Kingsley Publishers).
Here is a very witty and helpful book by a 13-year-old who has Asperger's Syndrome. After reading this book from cover to cover, I took it to several teacher/principal/parent meetings we had when dealing with bullying at the Junior High. I'm getting ready to ask Jon to read this one. Although we've always tried to explain autism to him, maybe in Luke's book he will see some similarities to himself, and it will get the conversation started. Because no matter how many times we've gone through it, nothing has really *clicked* in his understanding.

Asperger's and Self-Esteem: Insight and Hope Through Famous Role Models, by Norm Ledgin (2002, Future Horizons).
Mr. Ledgin takes us back through the lives of several famous people, Jefferson, Mozart, and Einstein to name a few, and points out the possible finding of autism/Asperger's traits. You will have to read this one to form your own conclusions, but one thing I came away with was the fact that most of our geniuses had problems with social skills or were antisocial. Does this place them on the spectrum? I don't know. I do know that sometimes it takes antisocial behavior to be able to isolate oneself, and create, invent, or do research. I myself need quiet and alone time as I write these words. The phone rings, Jon comes into the room and I get upset. This doesn't make me autistic, but for the moment I *want* to be antisocial. This book was very thought-provoking.

Succeeding in College with Asperger Syndrome: A Student Guide, by John Harpur, Maria Lawlor and Michael Fitzgerald (2003, Jessica Kingsley Publishers).
I've read through the opening chapters of this book, about preparing for college, sources of information, and making the right choice. This is one that I will read and have my son read as he gets closer to making this decision. Honestly, the reason I got this book was to prove to myself that, yes, it is possible to have HF autism/Asperger's and attend a college. So, if Jon really wishes to attend college, right here is where we can find

information to help us. And isn't it amazing that once again, UK publishers are there before us, anticipating our needs as parents.

The Disabled and Their Parents: A Counseling Challenge, by Leo Buscaglia (1983, SLACK).
This is a jewel of a book written by the author of *Love* and *Living, Loving and Learning*. After having read several books by Buscaglia, I was curious to find this one. After searching far and wide, I was unable to find it (alas, even the internet didn't turn it up). Imagine my delight when I found it at the bottom of a bag of books donated to the library book sale. Since I was the Library Director, it was in my authority to "shop" before the sale—thus, the book is now mine. If you get a chance to find this one, it is worth a read. Buscaglia talks to us, the parents, as would a loving father to a distressed child. From Chapter 1 titled "A Handicap is Made, Not Born," to the final chapter, "Tomorrow's Challenge," you will not only come away educated and encouraged, but comforted!

Realizing the College Dream with Autism or Asperger Syndrome, by Ann Palmer (2005, Jessica Kingsley Publishers).
This book seems to be stuck like glue to my right hand. I carry it with me everywhere I go, and pass it around to every teachers' meeting, IEP meeting, or parent group I attend. I had the pleasure of meeting Ann personally at a national Autism Society of America conference one summer. Not only is she a wonderful source of information, but her son, Eric, and my Jon, seem very similar—that is, both would rather be alone than in a group and both have college aspirations. We recently had another transition meeting, planning for a job during the summer and planning on a Junior College at first. Ann's book is what I'm living by at the moment.

This chapter on resources is inevitably short because these are resources that have helped *me*. There are hundreds of books, websites, and organizations out there on autism and Asperger's Syndrome. It is my hope that you not only find help here, but out there as well. Read a lot, research more, and as always, if it sounds too good to be true, it probably is! Don't forget to have a healthy dose of skeptic optimism, to keep you and your teenager safe.

Will I ever be able to stop searching for information?

chicken nugget #15

"We must see differently!"

Too much light often blinds gentlemen of this sort. They cannot see the forest for the trees.

(Christopher Martin Wieland 1768)

Does looking at our children in a certain way affect their lives?

When Jon reached his teens, we began thinking about pre-college classes, technical school, and job interests (be still, my fearful heart!). Jon expressed a desire to be a computer animator. So, I dutifully got online and did a search to find out exactly what he would need to know if he really wanted to pursue this as a career. I was not surprised to see several years of beginning drawing classes suggested before computer animation classes ever entered the picture. As a result, Jon agreed to take basic drawing instruction, one on one, from a good friend of ours.

We were in our fourth week, and I was wondering who was learning more, Jon or I. He has learned how to hold a charcoal pencil two different ways. How to try to pay attention to 45 minutes of instruction. How to make mistakes on the page and try not to care. And to my surprise, when he was practicing at home, he drew step by step George Washington's head, and I could instantly see from across the room that it indeed was Washington!

I have learned that no matter how many times my son tries things, and quits them, it is best that I allow him to keep trying new things. I have learned that my son does indeed, unlike his mother, have a talent for drawing. And I have come to realize that, sometimes, we need to learn to *see* differently.

As I sit and watch my son watch the teacher, she asks him repeatedly, "Can you see?" As in, can you see the line here? Can you see this shape or shading here? I'm in the room strictly to help or encourage him to pay attention and try to help him stay out of what he and I refer to as "la la land" (inattention), but I'm beginning to see certain things too.

I see my son, now a teenager, wearing braces for the past two months, as a gangly, self-conscious youth. I see when he gets frustrated, and I see when he is actually, honest to goodness, getting it!

As he draws and progresses with his drawing, I see that he is learning to see differently. He is seeing the lines, the shapes, and even the shading, instead of only the object that needs to be drawn. He may not have the technique down yet on how to get it onto the page, but he is seeing it.

I am seeing the man I hope he becomes, 20-something, able to work in some type of job, computer animation, drawing, or perhaps drafting. Instead of only seeing my son, I am seeing the shape of things to come. Instead of seeing the autism that at times controls my son, I'm seeing his successes in spite of his autism. In fact, I am seeing Jon controlling autism.

When I was teaching a creative writing class I mentioned on one occasion that I had always wanted to draw, but in seventh grade a teacher told me to change my goals since I didn't have a knack for drawing. I was devastated, but it was then that I began to write, so wasn't this really a good thing?

After class, one of my very talented students, both in writing and drawing, came up to me and asked me what I wanted to draw.

I waved my hand. "Oh, you know…like that tree out there," I said, indicating a bare winter oak.

She looked at the tree, back at me, and said, "You can draw that Mrs. Boushéy. You just have to draw what you *see*, not draw what you think you *should* see."

Ah ha… I thought about this for a long time. I even repeated it to my husband who nodded his head in his absentminded way. But it wasn't until this drawing class with Jon that I understood what my student meant. To be able to draw, you have to draw what you see, line by line, not draw the picture it already is. You have to see not only the trees in the forest, but also the individual shapes of those trees, down to the tiniest detail.

Thus, I believe we need to learn to see people with disabilities differently too. We need to stop seeing the already formed picture of the disability, and see that person as just a person in that moment of time.

When I go to pick up Jon at school, I park in our designated spot, at the top corner of the parking lot. On this day I am stuck in between several cars with moms waiting for their kids. As Jon makes his way up the steps to the top tier of parking I see that he is either talking to himself or singing to himself. Once the school bell rings and he gathers his stuff he usually goes straight to a video or a movie in his head, and this is where his focus is on the way out the door. On this particular day I also notice a girl walking parallel to him, heading for the mom and the car parked beside me. As Jon gets in on his side of the car, I glance over and watch the girl get into the car to my left. She motions to Jon and taps the side of her head, explaining something to her mom. Then she notices me watching and they both quickly look away.

Unfortunately I know what was probably being said. She was pointing my son out to her mom and tapping the side of her head, meaning he had something up with his brain. Hopefully she wasn't saying he was a nutcase, or crazy, but I get the picture from her actions. She was seeing the disability, autism, instead of seeing my son.

Jon chatters all the way home from school about what homework he has, but I can't get that picture out of my head, the girl tapping her head. Yes, kids are cruel. Hadn't I learned that well enough during the terror of Junior High? Yet it depressed me that another child was pointing my son out to her mom in this way. "Him? He's got a problem." Tap, tap. "Up here."

Of course I didn't say anything to Jon, except to remind him to try not to talk to himself as he's walking, because people will wonder about him. In fact, I told no one. It hurt too much then, and in fact still hurts.

But this is what I hope—I hope that not only I, but others, will learn to see Jon as a gangly teen with braces, concentrating on life; not as a teenager struggling with autism. If I can be the first to see the lines of the branch instead of the tree, then perhaps others will follow my lead. If I truly believe we must see differently, then it must start with me.

How can I work to change other people's eyesight as well?

Chapter Sixteen

Explaining their differences to our teens

Do I tell my son or daughter that they have autism or Asperger's? If so, when and how?

When he began High School, ninth grade, Jon was asked to attend his first IEP meeting. The rules and regulations read that anyone over 14 must attend these meetings to have input, when appropriate. Up to this point we had always said it was not appropriate for Jon to attend. I mean who would want to make their child sit in on an IEP meeting? That child is talked about in the third person—Jon is doing this, not this, etc.—and how would that be a benefit to the child? However, this was the start of High School and I didn't want to belabor the point, so all three of us showed up that first month of school to talk with his teachers.

Things began by the caseworker asking all of the teachers to take turns telling Jon how he was doing in their class. They proceeded to do this, and at first we thought Jon was tuning out, but then he interrupted his English teacher to point out that, yes, he had told her good morning, but it had only been one time. She had been pointing out that he was friendly and polite and told her good morning when he entered her class. Ha! He had been listening.

Then, just before Jon was to be excused so we could get down to discussing his IEP, the caseworker said, "What we are trying to do is try to see Jon, not his disability, and work with his personality, not necessarily the disability." I inwardly cringed. She was talking about my son's disability, in front of him. Did he catch that word?

Later on, my husband said he noticed it too, and pointed out that we needed to speak to her so she would be more careful. After all, we didn't want him to begin thinking that there was something wrong with him. I quickly agreed.

But you see, we are in a dilemma here because there is something wrong with him, isn't there? He has a disability called autism.

Again I racked my brain, trying to decide how to handle this, and I asked myself the following questions: Do we tell him he has autism? If so, when and how?

To be honest, this wasn't the first time I had tried to answer these questions. Several years back I attended a MAAP conference (More Advanced Autistic Persons) and had the pleasure of listening to a panel of young adults who happened to be on the autism spectrum. One young man named Paul McDonald commented that it wasn't until he understood his disability that he felt comfortable with himself. To him it was an Ah-ha moment, because now he understood why he was the way he was. He advised parents to give their children this information as soon as they could, to help them.

So, returning home from this conference, I discussed it with my husband and explained to him that we needed to try to help Jon understand this thing called autism. He agreed, and the following day while in the car I tried explaining to Jon what autism was. I told him it was the way a person's brain developed and that his brain developed differently from mine. I explained that when he thinks, he *sees* what he is thinking, like when he told me what he sees when he thinks about a dog—his first picture, the orange dog in Dr. Seuss's *Go Dog Go*, next picture, of his Uncle's dog. I told him my brain wasn't like that. I did not think in pictures. He also has an amazing memory, where he is able to record and remember entire videos. I couldn't do that either, and this was autism. He said, okay. He was 11 at the time.

But did he get it? Did he have that Ah-ha moment and suddenly understand why he is the way he is? No, I sincerely doubt it, because every year since then I've had the same conversation with him. Trying to explain how people are different, and he is different. His brain developed differently, and this is autism. This is why he has an aide to help him keep things together at school and other students don't have this luxury. This is why he feels *different* from other kids. This is why he comments that he likes *different* things than other kids. I use the d-word as in different, but I have never used the d-word as in disability. Is this perhaps why he isn't understanding autism? Do I have to explain to him what a disability is for him to understand autism?

How many parents, and educators for that matter, since working with a child on the autism spectrum, have told the child they are disabled? Okay. I sincerely doubt that there was a show of hands. Any disability can be devastating and debilitating. Once we've come to accept that our child needs help, do we then work at getting the child to understand they are disabled?—A thousand times NO!

Our job as parents is to support, help, advocate for our child, not pound into their head that they are disabled. From day one, life becomes a struggle not only for our child, but for us, as *we* fight against the *theys* of the world who can't get past our child's disability. Why would we even want to go there when we are trying so hard to get past there?

In Luke Jackson's book, *Freaks, Geeks and Asperger Syndrome*, which he wrote as a young teenager, he states: "One unusual thing about me is that I have what some people would call a disability but I call a gift—Asperger Syndrome" (Jackson 2002, p.19). I read his book and I wonder how he came to his Ah-ha moment? How did his parents get him to realize, rethink, and accept this fact of life? I must admit that I am stumped.

Looking online at the expert and parent opinions, I find an article titled *Getting Started: Introducing Your Child to His or Her Diagnosis of Autism or Asperger Syndrome* (Wheeler 2004). Written by Marci Wheeler, a social worker at the Indiana Resource Center for Autism, it directly tries to answer my why? when? and how? questions.

The why? restates what I had already known, that most autistic or Asperger's adults say they wish they had been told earlier about their disability. She points out that several adults didn't know growing up that they had a disability and as a result grew up thinking they were stupid or lazy, thus developing very low self-esteem. She believes that the child, even a child on the autism spectrum, can sense the "frustration and confusion" which may surround them, and if someone doesn't try to give them a logical reason, they become frustrated and confused themselves.

The when? she admits is not exact, since every child's ability and level of understanding affects this. Some do not get a diagnosis until later in life, especially those who may be high-functioning, or would fall into Asperger's Syndrome. She points out that some children, especially during the teen years may ask, "Why can't I be like everyone else?" or "What is wrong with me?" This is a good time to tackle this information as long as it's done in a positive way, and here, she and I totally agree. She writes: "A positive attitude about *differences* can be established"

(Wheeler 2004, p.2, emphasis added). Not disability mind you, but differences, as in, everyone is unique and has different abilities.

The how? she explains must also be individualized. Some children need very little information to begin with. They only wish a simple answer to their questions. Some are ready and capable to do reading themselves, and she points out that there are several books out there, which are good for this. *Freaks, Geeks and Asperger Syndrome* by Luke Jackson is the one I've been reading through and am thinking about passing on to Jon.

Wheeler takes this discussion one step further and comes to a who? and where? Here she says will be another individualized choice. She states that some parents ask for this information to be given to their child from a specialist, someone outside the family unit. She explains that receiving this information will be very troubling and confusing and that the child will need the parents to play a supportive role instead of the role of the informer.

I move from Wheeler's article to essays and postings by parents. It seems I am not the only one who has raised this question. A father, Dave Ingold, writes an article for the Autism Society of Wisconsin newsletter titled *How Do I Tell My Child About His [Her] Diagnosis?* (1999, p.1). His six steps of suggestions are similar to Wheeler's and very practical. A few things he points out stay with me.

He states, "Kids can be pretty resilient, as long as they're told…that a 'condition' is how things are, and that anything that they want to do or be is achievable, just by using different methods from what they have been trying." He also points out what I always try to get through to others, we are not alone in this situation. We should continually try to connect not only with experts in the field, but with other parents who have been through and are going through the same thing. Looking at the pages of information I was able to print down on this topic alone, proves this point. We don't have to try to answer all of the questions ourselves. There is nothing wrong with looking to others.

The last thing Mr. Ingold points out is short and to the point. He states at the end of his list, "Go to step one. Remember the shampoo instructions? Lather, Rinse, Repeat?" (1999, p.5). Humorous, but right on target!

When my first book, *Parent to Parent*, came out, I went around to booksellers, introduced myself, and left them marketing packets. After all, if I didn't tell them about my book and try to encourage them to place it on their shelves, who would? Jon went with me as I made the rounds, since he loves bookstores.

A week later I got a call from a local store manager. After speaking to her for a while, she became more excited about my book, and explained that her child had an ADD diagnosis. She said that my book would also be relevant to her, and not only was she going to order it for the store, but also a copy for herself.

This particular store is Jon's favorite large bookstore, so when I picked him up from school I told him that in a week my book would be on the shelf there. He asked, "What is your book about again?" I was momentarily speechless. Jon had lived through the first writing, almost step by step. He had donated the jokes for the chapter on humor. I had explained to him more than several times what the book was about.

I took Dave Ingold's advice. Just like the instructions on the shampoo bottle. I told Jon that the book was about him and autism. "You remember, I explained what autism is?"

"No," he said.

"It's the way your brain has developed differently than other people's brains. It's why you have a great memory and I don't. It's why you may need extra help by having a helper in school where other students don't, but it also means your computer skills are great compared to some kids."

"Oh, okay," came his reply.

Did he have that Ah-ha moment? Probably not. Did he understand any more than he had before? Maybe. It's difficult to tell how much our children really take in. After reading up on this subject, looking at what the experts and other parents have to say, do I feel our children *should* be told about their autism or Asperger's? Several parents said they did not want their child to have to carry a label around with them while growing up, and the less explained, the better.

In my first book I visited a topic on looking at autism not as a disability but as a culture. As with that discussion, this one too, has several pros and cons. I admitted to sitting on the fence on that one, encouraging parents and educators to read, study, and come to their own conclusions. I must admit that the fence is a good place for me on this one too.

Yes, I've tried to explain to Jon about autism. But I really don't think it is getting through. No, I do not want to explain to him what a disability is unless it becomes necessary. One day he may have his Ah-ha moment. I hope to be available to help him at that time.

Yesterday I felt I should explain to him, again, what my book is about. But today, I don't even want to mention to him that he is different from other kids. What has happened in that 24 hours?—His friend, who happens to be a girl, can't come to his birthday party. He is feeling down, and low, and explaining differences to him is not going to help him deal with his teenage sense of rejection.

Instead I said, "Well, you know, Jon. Girls are funny sometimes. One day you are their friend and the next day you are not. Julie is a nice girl. But don't take it too hard. She may talk to you again in the hall next week. And anyway, girls are interested in girl things you know…" He listens, nods his head, and swipes at a tear. And I end up trying to explain another truth to him. Girls are *different*.

Being a former teenage girl myself, I think they should come with their own label, and maybe a sticker for their forehead stating, "I'm a teenage girl! I am having a bad day/week/month. Give me some space!"

Maybe I will use this example the next time Jon and I talk about differences. She is a girl, you are a boy. She is moody, you are, hmmm, autistic? "Vive la différence!"

Why can't we just erase the word "disability" when talking about autism?

chicken nugget #16

Thoughts on normal

Lately my thoughts have turned to normal. Not that my thoughts were abnormal, but thoughts on being normal. The *New York Times* published an article one day titled "For Families of Autistic, the Fight for Ordinary." I received an e-mail from a writer friend living in upstate New York telling me I should read the article. He also added that after reading it he felt he understood a little better what my life was like with my son. I hurried to the library the next day and was able to print the article down from the internet.

In it, the writer Jane Gross interviews several parents like myself, living and working with autistic children. One parent is getting her daughter painstakingly ready to receive her first communion. Another talks about the intense planning it takes to even go for haircuts. At one point Gross states, "It is a relentless, labor-intensive and harrowing task, overwhelmingly performed by mothers, that tests the strength of marriages, the resilience of siblings and the endurance of the women themselves…"

What task is Gross referring to at this point? The struggle of living with an autistic child? No. In this case she is talking about the struggle or fight, as she calls it, "for *Ordinary*."

I read through this article, read it to my husband and wonder who else I can share it with? This is so typical of our life too, it is almost as if Gross, writing from New York, has featured our mid-western family as well.

We too had to plan extensively for Jon's first haircut. Actually, this wasn't really his first, after all he was ten and my husband had been cutting Jon's hair up to that point, but this was his first outside haircut we attempted in a long, long time. I asked the lady who did my own hair, if she would do my son's. Of course she said yes, and I then gave her a few more details about Jon. The fact that he couldn't stand the water sprayed on his head. The fact that he was a little afraid of the electric trimmer. And the fact that he may say things that may be too blunt, or to the point, but to please not take it personally. (As in, "Oh no! What did you do to my hair?")

After much preparation also on Jon's part—please try to sit still; you know it doesn't hurt, Dad cuts your hair all of the time (although Dad did nick a squirming Jon on the ear once)—we arrived at the salon. Lynn and Jon seemed to hit it off and I took myself over to a corner, to let him try to handle things on his own. I noticed that he was telling her a Disney video, from beginning to end of course, and Lynn was a-humming and listening and cutting away on his hair. All too soon, she used an oversized pastry brush on the back of his neck and he was done.

"But I didn't get to finish!" he protested.

"That's okay, Jon," she said. "Just remember where you were for next time."

This seemed to satisfy him. And sure enough, he did remember where he was four months later, and four months after that. Thus, we learned how to get a haircut. Find him someone with a sympathetic ear and let him tell a story while they cut away. It still works to this day.

We have also handled dentist visits in this way and even eating out. If Jon can tell a story to someone, the dental assistant, or us at the table while waiting for food, he can handle the situation he is in. We use his habit of repeating stories (see chicken nugget #6 on perseveration) to keep him calm and happy in a situation that may not have normally worked for him.

And now I'm back to discussing normal. With trial and error, Jon has learned to sit for a haircut and the dentist (even the orthodontist!). With understanding on our part, we can help him keep busy while we wait in restaurants or long lines. We have been able to create *moments of normal* for him. Anyone who may look our way sees a family of three, the son talking the parents ear off, but otherwise pretty normal.

I think about normal right now not only because of the article in the *New York Times*, but because we recently made Jon spend the night at his cousins' house. These are girl cousins, younger than he and a little bit wild as girls can be. He called us six times that night, pleading with us to come and pick him up. He was uncomfortable, dreading sleeping. His last call was at 11:00p.m. and I told him we were going to bed, he should go to bed too. He would be fine. Good night.

He was fine. He didn't like it, but he had a normal night, sleeping over at someone else's home. He realized he could do it after doing it, and I realized he could do it too.

Why did we force him to stay overnight someplace else? Because it was good for him. Because he needs to learn to trust other people and trust himself alone with other people. And because we are always pursuing moments of *normal*.

This year we will travel the furthest we've ever been as a family for vacation—destination Hawaii. Not only because it's a once-in-a-lifetime trip for us, but because it will give Jon more opportunities to experience normal. I look forward to it with excitement and a little trepidation, always hoping for a *normal* vacation.

Chapter Seventeen

A case for empathy

Great persons are able to do great kindness.

(Cervantes 1605)

If the experts say people with autism are unable to show empathy or compassion, how is it that my son's life proves differently?

I started discussing this notion of empathy, or lack thereof, very early on. I had read everything I could get my hands on, and in several books had found discussions on "theory of mind." In Bryna Siegel's groundbreaking book *The World of the Autistic Child* (1996, p.28) she states that the theory of mind is "the capacity to understand that others think the same way you do... Autistic and PDD children are very slow to develop even a partial theory of mind, and many never really develop it at all" (p.28). She explains that this is why their social skills are so impaired, and if they are verbal, their social language. They have difficulty reading body language, and thus any social cues in the situation. Which is why the concept of someone being sarcastic needs to be taught, as well as figuring out when someone is joking, serious, or maybe being hateful. They won't "get it" the way neurotypical kids do.

This lack of theory of mind, being able to understand how others may be thinking, even feeling, then rolls over to the inability to be empathetic towards another person. Empathy, compassion, sympathy—they all go hand and hand, and we find that the experts believe our children are incapable of these feelings. Most recently I found a study by a group of Dutch scientists as reported on the BBC News website, titled *Empathy Finding Offers Autism Hope*. This article defines a study about doing brain scans to see which areas of the brain light up during certain thinking processes. They found that a certain area, the motor system, lights up when we predict the actions of others and when we plan our own actions. They report that the brain develops this ability to predict others' actions in two ways, one through "theory of mind" (understanding another's possible thoughts) and the other being a "simulation theory." This simulation theory is the idea that actions, of how to react to someone else, are actions that are learned and thus can be taught. They now believe that just as we teach good manners, we can teach appropriate reactions in social situations and thus simulate appropriate feelings such as empathy. The report ends up by quoting one of the researchers who states: "However…this was not possible for *the truly autistic person*, as for them another person doesn't exist at all" (Ramani 2004).

Before my son even carried this diagnosis of autism, I noticed that he was a very empathetic child. One day we were in the grocery store behind a woman who had a very obvious skin rash on her legs. Even I noticed it was nasty, swollen-looking, and that her legs seemed to be completely covered. I had almost forgotten six-year-old Jon was standing in line next to me until he said, "Look Mommie," pointing at the lady's legs.

"Shh…I know, I see," I told him, trying to distract his attention. But before I knew it he had tapped her on the arm.

"Does it hurt?" he asked.

I immediately felt embarrassed and told him not to bother her. She didn't hear him and turned around and smiled at us. I pulled him back next to me and smiled back.

"Shh…," I whispered to him. "Don't bother her."

"It hurts," he added and began to cry.

I knelt down beside him. "It's okay. See, she's okay."

"It hurts," was all he could repeat.

Several years after diagnosis, and several books and articles later telling me that my son would not be able to show empathy, his fourth grade teacher broke her leg in an accident. She continued to come to school, first using crutches and then limping in a walking cast. One day there was a note in Jon's daily communication notebook that Jon was complaining of leg pain. His aide had taken him to the nurse and was unable to see any bruises or find out if he had hurt himself on the playground or not. The aide wanted me to be aware so we could look into it. That evening I asked him probably the same questions the nurse had asked—did you fall on the playground, did you twist it somehow? When all answers produced a no, I decided it was nothing major and told him he would soon be better.

The next day, another note came home saying that Jon had started limping, saying his leg still hurt. This time I called the teacher and caught her before she had gone home for the day. After a few minutes of discussion and going over the fact that we both had again asked him the same questions, we realized that he must be having empathy pains for his teacher's broken leg. We laughed about it, but then decided that perhaps she should talk to him about it the next day at school.

That day, I went inside to wait for Jon and to speak to her about what had happened. She said she had talked to Jon about her leg and his leg and told him that her leg, wrapped up in the cast, didn't hurt at all. She was limping because it was awkward to carry such a heavy cast around. She also pointed out that he didn't have a cast on his leg and his leg really should feel fine and he should be able to walk just fine. We decided to give it the weekend to see if this was empathy pains or really something wrong with his leg.

As we expected, by Sunday night, Jon was back to walking what was "normal" for him, his long loping gait, and said his leg didn't hurt any more. I sent this information in the communication notebook on Monday morning and wasn't surprised to see a note at the end of the day that said he hadn't complained of a leg ache all day and was back to his own walk.

My son is autistic. My son experienced empathy pains for his teacher. How do we explain that?

Recently as I prepared this chapter, I once again tried to find any information I could on autism and empathy. Most of the experts out there still say that empathy is associated with theory of mind. And since it is difficult for autistics to "mind read" or understand how another person could be thinking or feeling, they will indeed have trouble expressing empathy.

Yet my son worries constantly about his older grandmother, living alone, an hour north of us. Every time she gets sick, he asks if she is dying. When she gets a cold, he wants to call her all the time and ask how she is doing. Empathy or just worry?

This past week he and I were talking about the importance of socializing and caring about people instead of things. (We have this conversation constantly, trying to get it to sink in, knowing that he is not only autistic but probably an introvert too.) Jon interrupted me this time and said, "But Mom, I care how other people feel. If someone is sick or hurt, it bothers me." I had to agree with him, knowing that this was a fact.

So how do we explain this empathy my son has, coming from someone who is not supposed to be able to have it?

Once again, it has to go on my "autism is a mystery" page. Not everything is known about this disability, because not everything is known about the way the brain functions. Listening to Dr. Temple Grandin speak at a conference once, I remember her talking about the library on her campus being flooded, and how she felt real pain for all of the books that were damaged, so much so that she got involved in the restoration process of trying to save them. She was excited that they could put the books into "cold storage" and try to get the moisture out of them that way. Someone raised their hand and asked if she felt this same pain when it came to dealing with people. Did she empathize with others? She thought for a moment and said, "Well, I do with cattle and livestock, and animals." Then she went off to talk about the squeeze machine she had developed to keep cattle calm while in holding pens for shots and branding.

She never really answered the question when it came to people, and I wonder if because autism is such an *individual* disability, do autistic individuals feel empathy only the way *they* can feel it? They empathize with something or someone they are closely connected to? Dr. Grandin, the books, and because of her job, livestock—my son, his teacher, and his grandmother? Of course this doesn't explain why Jon gets upset when he sees a total stranger who is hurting—and now we've come full circle.

Autism and empathy—will this question ever truly be answered?

chicken nugget #17

"But do I have to fix him?"

Do I have to fix him?

When Jon was just beginning to work with a speech therapist, and an occupational therapist at the schools, I remember one therapist in particular. She had just attended our first IEP meeting of the school year, had just met us and had been given a "mini-introduction to Jon session." She was very educated, and very enthusiastic about working with Jon, but when we walked out of the classroom, on the way down the hall, one thing she said stuck in my mind, and still does after all of these years: "I'm so glad to be working with Jon this year! I have so many plans for him. By the time he advances to the upper grades we are going to have him FIXED!"

I remember at the time laughing, and agreeing with her, even if I really didn't know exactly what she was getting at. Later, off and on during the week, her comment seemed to swirl around in my head, and I kept coming back to the same question. "Does Jon need to be fixed?"

I asked my husband how he felt about this.

"Well, you know what she meant," he said. "She meant that she can't wait to help him with his social skills, help him learn to get along at school so he will do better later."

Yes, I knew this was probably what she meant, but this is not what she said. She said she was excited about fixing Jon. Fixing, as in *broken*. My son was broken and needed to be fixed, repaired, mended, restored. Yes, I knew her intentions were good, but her comment drove me to distraction and wouldn't let me go.

As a matter of fact, since that day, it has still been driving me. In *Parent to Parent*, my first book, I wrote a short chapter addressing the issue of "autism as a culture." In that chapter I struggled with this idea of fixing, because if autism is a culture it's not the autistic person who needs to be fixed, it's the other people in the world who don't understand this different culture who need to make a correction. I wrote then that there were of course two sides to this very volatile topic, and now, several years later, it hasn't changed.

One side believes more or less that if you take away the autism, you take away the person. The other side believes that the autism needs to be removed so that the person can live a better life. But since there isn't a "cure" or magic pill to take away this autism, is this a moot point? I've always thought so, but recently I've been thinking a little differently. What's brought about this different way of thinking?—Research.

Research into the cause of autism seems to be getting closer and closer to an answer. I instinctively feel that my son's autism is closely related to genes. Scientists seem to be getting nearer to saying the same thing. As I begin to realize that Jon's autism was probably caused by our genes, I begin to wonder if there really is an answer to preventing other kids from being born this way. Once I wonder this, then I have to question if it's a good thing or a bad thing to have tests done during a pregnancy to search for any defect in the fetus. And if I go to that question, then I must go to the question of abortion and ethics and playing God. Oh my, what a can of worms one little question has caused!

On the website (home.att.net/~ascaris1) of Frank Klein, an adult on the spectrum, you can read several well-written essays on his opinions on this topic. At the bottom of his biography he states: "I want to get the word out that autism is not a disease to be cured, but is instead akin to being a totally different kind of person—one that thinks, acts, and learns differently than normal people, but is still fully equal." I read this and I totally agree with him.

But then I look at the sites posted by DAN, Defeat Autism Now, and CAN, Cure Autism Now, and see letters from parents who will try absolutely anything they can get their hands on to get rid of the autism in their child. And of course I agree with them too. How many times have I thought or even said, "If there was a way to get rid of the autism in Jon's life, I would be one of the first in line." Although Jon is considered high-functioning autistic, the autism is always there, on a daily basis, and this I hate.

So, here I am again. Straddling that fence I hopped up on in my first book in the chapter "Autism as a culture." Of course, I see both sides.

I understand what Frank is saying when he advises parents to see and love their child for who they are, autism and all. I understand too when he talks about the moral and ethical dilemma of genetic testing for autism and other forms of disability. These are all tough questions, Frank, ones that we must deal with individually, as we deal individually with God. There did not exist a test when I was pregnant with Jon to determine if he was genetically *whole*. If they developed one tomorrow, would I feel other parents should submit to such a test?

I know there are tests for several severe birth defects, and if the woman is older, these tests are recommended. I know that I wish no parent would go through life with a disabled child, no matter what the disability. I also know that Jon's place on the autism spectrum is difficult to deal with at times, and, yes, it could be much worse. So, am I advocating for genetic testing?—No. I'm advocating that the parent be allowed to have all of the information at hand and be able to make an informed, personal, and at times private, decision—hopefully, without judgment.

Lately I have also realized that, maybe, I don't want Jon to be a typical teenager. (Oh my gosh! Did I think or write that?) Yes. Lately, as Jon has entered High School I've noticed there are a lot of typical teens who I don't want to be around. Jon's cousin for one, seems to be having a rougher time than most, struggling with teenage attitude, rage, rebellion. Don't get me wrong, I see a lot of great teens out there too. But I've begun thinking maybe it's okay that Jon is the way he is. He still enjoys going to the movies with Mom and Dad. He is interested in girls, but isn't consumed by the thought of them yet. (At least I don't think he is.) He has fun, most of the time. Has a great sense of humor, and seems to be a happy youth. Stack those characteristics up against others, and those look pretty good.

But almost immediately after having these thoughts, we get an e-mail from a teacher explaining that Jon's attitude that day in class was a shock. He said he wasn't going to do his work, he didn't care to get any help and he shrugged his shoulders when the teacher tried to talk to him about it. After school I speak with Jon and his aide in the parking lot and find out that Jon didn't realize it was *work*. He thought it was extra credit, bonus work, and his attitude has always been, like most kids, if I don't have to do it, I'm not going to do it. "Oh," he told her. "I didn't realize I *had* to do it." So, on the way to school the next day we practice how to explain to this teacher that he misunderstood about the work. Jon also says he will try to remember to ask the speech teacher, who he sees once a week, to help him learn the difference between displaying good attitude and bad. Something he will have to learn, just like at times he had to learn scripted conversations.

Another fire put out. And I realize again, I hate this autism, no matter how high-functioning Jon is. I love *him*, but I *hate* this disability. If I could, I would fix him in a heartbeat. But I can't.

Surely there is a better word for what is needed? Repair, mend, restore, patch, straighten, place? Thats the one. I can't fix but I can touch up, make better, adjust, straighten, and, most importantly, *place him*. I can help Jon find his place, the right place, in this world, autism and all.

Since I can't fix him, is there a better way to place him?

Chapter Eighteen

The s-e-x word meets the
a-u-t-i-s-m word

I'd rather hit than have sex.

(Reggie Jackson, baseball great)

In the Spring a young man's fancy lightly turns to love.
(Tennyson 1842)

Just because my child is autistic, does this mean puberty will be delayed or different?

"Okay, you have got to hear about this," I tell my husband over the phone, making sure to speak in hushed tones. "I go on his computer just now and out of curiosity, I scroll through the history on the internet sites he has been visiting today. You will not believe it!" I pause and make sure my son is not listening at the door. "Pictures, pictures of naked women!"

"What?"

"Yup. And when I asked him what in the world he was doing? He said he was just searching on Google the phrase *huge muscle women* or *world's strongest women*. When I pointed out that each site sent him to naked women he covered his face and said, "I know! But I didn't look! I quickly clicked off the site!"

"How did he learn how to do that? And why was he doing that?" my husband asks.

I quickly remind him that Jon is a computer whiz and knows more about computers than the both of us.

"Didn't you have it locked with a password?"

Yes, I had forgotten to tell him about the password. I explain how I asked Jon just how he was able to search these sites. He had confessed, "I'm sorry Mom, but I figured out your password!"

By now, my husband is laughing and I am too—a little. When pushed to tell the truth, Jon will tell, even if it gets him into trouble, like now. I had already changed the password, had set the blocks on the computer to the most restrictive, and had told him he was not allowed to get on the internet when I was not at home.

To answer my husband's second question, "Why was he doing that?" Well, here we were, staring the truth of puberty in the face. After attending a conference on autism and puberty and reading the book *I Openers: Parents Ask Questions About Sexuality and Children with Developmental Disabilities* (Hingsberger 1993), I knew Jon would hit it soon, right along with his peers, but with him being our only child, my husband and I didn't know what to expect. We were now finding out.

After this first incident with the pictures on the computer I told my husband that he had to talk to his son. He had to remember how he was when he was 14, and he had to have a father–son talk with Jon. After a few days passed, he did, and although I wasn't privy to what went down, he said that Jon had some really amazing questions which he'd tried to answer the best he could, along with the assurance that Jon could come talk to him at any time about anything.

This all sounded good. I knew my son was going through puberty, I knew he suddenly had sex and naked women on the brain, even if he didn't understand it all, but I didn't want to have to be the one to talk to him about it.

Not too much later the next problem that came up was self-gratification, the M-word. Once again, I told my husband he had to talk to him. We believe that masturbation is normal, a puberty thing, but he needed to know he couldn't do it in public, or constantly, or when he was around other people.

My husband had another talk. This one slightly more explicit, and I definitely didn't want to know the details of this one.

All seemed to be calming down on the puberty front until one week when my husband was out of town. I had to take Jon into the office with me, and several times I caught him doing what he was not supposed to be doing in a public place. Granted, we own our own business so I was the only one there at the time, but this was a public place.

After the third time in an eight-hour day I decided that his dad's talk hadn't worked. So on the way home from work (we have our best conversations in the car), I laid it out for him.

"Okay, Jon. You know you have a penis. You know it feels good to play with, but you can't be playing with it all of the time, especially in public places, around other people or any place other than the privacy of your bedroom or the bathroom at home."

Jon covered his face in embarrassment. "Okay, you caught me red-handed." (How appropriate, I thought!) "It's just that it relaxes me," he explained.

"Okay. But you can't do it out in public and you can't be doing it *constantly*. So you have a penis, get over it, and stop focusing on it and doing what you are doing!" He assured me he heard me this time and he would stop doing it "all the time."

Later, when my husband got home, I repeated what I had said. He looked at me in surprise.

"I had to be blunt with him," I said. "And maybe he heard us this time?"

It's six months now after that conversation, and is the problem solved? Well, I know that he is not "doing it all the time" or around me and his dad. Has he gotten over his interest in sex and girls? Do normal kids get over it?

It's a very private and touchy subject, puberty. So why do I put it out here, on the page—in a book? Because if we, as parents, don't talk about it, we will all be asking ourselves the same questions, and never getting any answers because we are afraid, ashamed, or too shy to discuss it. Yes, our children, sons and daughters, will be maturing and going through puberty usually right along with the rest of their peers. Yes, we may have to deal with it a little differently and tailor all discussions and information to meet our individual child's needs. In the end, your child will be better for the open communication. And if all else fails, just lay down the law as I had to. Most of our kids are very particular in following rules.

An interesting note, the same summer my son discovered naked women he acquired a compulsive interest in all things *Muppets*. Yes, the Muppets, as in the videos and the TV series. So while we were locking his computer to cut out possible naked women sites, we were tracking down all of the Muppet shows.

I had another Ah-ha moment.

This is what autism is. My son is going through puberty and is interested in the Muppets at the same time. This is the imbalance, which the experts talk about, things in his life not developing at an even rate. He had his first crush on a girl last year and wanted her for a girlfriend, but they had nothing to talk about, because she wasn't interested in *Power Rangers*. I felt sorry for him and so did his speech teacher. She ended up writing little scripted conversations for him so he could learn Junior High small talk.

Did it work?—He feels more comfortable now talking to this girl, but one day when I picked him up from school and asked what Carole had to say today, he said, "I sat next to her in the morning but I didn't talk to her 'cause I didn't want the other kids to think I liked her."

Ah yes, I remember doing that! Puberty has definitely hit. Do I wish for my son to rather hit a baseball than have sex, as Reggie Jackson said. No. I know Reggie was talking about abstinence before a game to keep in form. But to me, this hitting the ball instead could mean the distance Jon always puts between himself and others. Puberty is not fun, relationships will be very challenging for my son. But I would much rather he go through the whole thing along with his peers. And although I may yet feel uncomfortable with the topic, I am his mother, and I'm in it for the long haul.

I wonder if an autistic or Asperger's daughter would be easier at this age?

chicken nugget #18

Waiting for the other shoe to drop—optimistically being pessimistic

Have you ever heard the story about the "other shoe"? A couple have been married for a long time. The husband works nights and comes in around one in the morning. The wife has gotten so used to this over the years, that she dozes off and on until he gets home, but doesn't really sleep until he is in bed. One night the man comes in from work and proceeds to get ready for bed. The wife settles into the gentle rhythm of his routine. She hears him down the hall brushing his teeth and gargling. Finished, he enters the bedroom and she feels the bed sag as he sits down to remove his shoes. This takes some time as he has gotten a little stout, and it's more difficult for him to reach the laces. The bed creaks, one shoe gently plops onto the carpet. She imagines him pulling off the sock and she waits for the movement towards the other shoe. The bed shifts again. She waits again. There is no corresponding plop.

Where is that other shoe she thinks? She waits a few more seconds, hearing his breathing as he sits on the side of the bed. The shoe doesn't drop. Something is very wrong, she thinks. She sits up and switches on the lamp. He is sitting with his head in his hands. This can't be good. "What is it?" she whispers.

"Honey, I've just been laid off from the job."

She moves closer and places a hand on his arm. "I knew something was wrong…I've been lying here all this time waiting for the other shoe to drop!"

The expression *waiting for the other shoe to drop* has come to mean, waiting for—anticipating—bad news. Which it seems is what I've been doing for about a week.

Jon is now in full swing at High School, about one month into the first semester. There have already been ups and downs, his adjustment and mine. We continue to take it one day at a time. Last week was our first scheduled IEP meeting with all of his teachers invited to come. As usual, doing my normal thing, I began stressing about it, and planning for it, about a week before.

High School and High School teachers are totally different from anything we have ever dealt with. At one time I was a full-time substitute teacher for both area High Schools. I know what this age group is like. I was very familiar with the environment and knew what it was like for a High School teacher trying to deal with High School students either typical or non-typical.

Thus, I carried several preconceived ideas before the semester even began, and most of them were not positive. How was my autistic son, high-functioning or not, going to be able to take on High School? High School meant independence, friends, after-school activities, jobs, driving, teenage hormones, tough love from the teachers. How would Jon be able to handle all of this?

These questions and more began swirling through my head, keeping me awake at night. So I did what works best for me. I got on the internet and did a search for any new information on High School students and autism. I found several very informative articles, one titled *Asperger's Students in High School* by Leslie S. Klein, PhD (2002). She not only gives parents and educators tips on what we should be doing at this time, but she points out a few expectations the Asperger's student may have, things Jon may be expecting.

- High School teachers will know him as well as previous teachers had known him.

- The special arrangements made for him will continue in his new school.

- He will be interacting with a small number of teachers/aide/administrators.

- The schedule will apply forever, there will not be any unexpected changes.

- (Wish) Students will not see him as different.

- (Fear) Students will see him as different.

- Others will adapt to his personality (peculiarities, obsessions, rigidity).

- Parents will be able to intervene as effectively as they had in elementary school (Klein 2002, p.1).

After reading through this list, it seemed like a light went on inside my head. This was probably what my Jon had been going through this past month. Not only did we, his parents and teachers, have expectations of him, but he had expectations of himself for others. Some were easier to deal with, like the High School teachers getting to know him. (I had already given them an "Introduction to Jon" letter.) However, a few of the other items on the list such as, *wishing* the students would not see him as different, *fearing* that they will, were a little more complicated and not easily fixable.

I printed the article by Dr. Klein, along with two others. One by Dr. Temple Grandin on *Teaching Tips for Children and Adults with Autism* (2004) and another found on www.teacch.com titled *Recommendations for Students with High Functioning Autism* (Hogan n.d.). Thus armed, my husband and I showed up bright and early on a Thursday morning for our first High School IEP meeting.

I was happy to see that all of his teachers had been able to come, except one, so there were nine educators and my husband and I. Sitting down at the table, the first item of note was that the meeting would be a quick 15–20 minutes as the teachers needed to get to class to start their day. "Okay," I thought. "So much for any intense discussion." I quickly passed out the articles I had brought, explaining that I never wanted to ask a teacher to do something that was not doable, so I had found several good articles to help us, and asked them to read them at their leisure.

Because Jon had been invited to the first half of the meeting (for the first time), we then proceeded around the table rather quickly, giving each teacher a chance to tell Jon what he was doing which was positive in their classroom. About six minutes later, he was asked if he had anything to add? He said no, and asked if he could leave and go shelve books, and was told he could. I was actually very proud of him for sitting through a somewhat uncomfortable situation and listening to nine teachers talk about him.

We discussed a few minor issues, continuing social goals and a few ongoing challenges, like keeping his homework planner organized. Then, true to her word, the caseworker wrapped it up and dismissed the meeting about 25 minutes later. The meeting was short, to the point, and very efficient. My husband and I sat for a few more minutes, spoke with the special services autism coordinator and Jon's speech teacher, and were on our way.

The over-all consensus? Jon was doing very well. A great start to High School. A few things still needed to be worked out. His teachers were getting to know him and he them, but so far, so good.

We were quiet in the car on the way to the office. I asked my husband what he thought. "Well, so far, so good," he echoed. "The caseworker this year seems very together. I thought she was the High School Principal at first, until I realized she was the caseworker."

I too felt relief that the meeting had gone so well and that the caseworker seemed so on top of things compared to the past two years. But there was something niggling at me. Something swirling at the back of my mind.

A week passed and one morning I woke up with a thought! Things had gone *too smoothly*.

This first IEP meeting which I had stressed about for a week or more, had gone off without a hitch. All of his nine teachers were happy, the caseworker was happy. We came away happy. Where was the struggle like we had gone through in Junior High? This time I didn't come away with a feeling of we vs. they, which had been the typical outcome during Junior High meetings. As a matter of fact when I got to the office the morning after the meeting, I sent the caseworker an e-mail telling her that we now felt Jon had another advocate, someone in his corner, besides his parents working with him, and I thanked her.

Why did any of this bother me?

Writer Ruth Rendell says: "While most of the things you've worried about have never happened, it's a different story with the things you haven't worried about. They are the ones that happen."

Funny, but in my case, too true. Not only have I been Jon's mom and advocate his entire life, but I'm his worrier. I worry about an issue, get stressed about it, and then (a) read up on it, (b) try to fix it, or (c) find out why I can't do (a) or (b). This is how I go through life, not only with Jon and autism, but everything. Now, things were going smoothly. At the moment there was nothing to (a), (b), and (c) about!

What am I to do? I'm waiting for the other shoe to drop. That other shoe was what was niggling me, swirling in the back of my mind. I'm usually a very optimistic person, so do I feel that this is turning me into a pessimist?—Not one bit.

I'm *optimistically* waiting for bad news, expecting that other shoe… and for some reason, in realizing this, I now feel so much better! Bring it on!

Chapter Nineteen
Charting behaviors

Nothing is permanent but change.

(Heraclitus c.500 BC, Greek philosopher)

Now that my son is older, do I see any changes in his autistic-like behavior?

Change is inevitable, change for the better, and for the worse. When my son was young and just diagnosed, I used to watch him like a hawk, trying to detect changing behavior, for the worse. Then I realized that I couldn't live with that daily fear, so I tried to teach myself to live in the moment and take his changes one day at a time. (Yes, still working on that one!) But it does help to remind myself that all kids change, neuro-typicals as well as developmentally disabled. My son's changes will not be like any other child's and vice versa. I have a nephew who has hit puberty and become a teenager with a bang. Suddenly he dislikes everyone and doesn't need *anyone's* help for *anything*. I certainly hope he gets through this stage quick because one of the adults who is dealing with his attitude may just decide he needs it adjusted. Although my son is also changing, has changed—and he and this nephew are the exact same age—because of autism, Jon's changes are totally unique to himself.

Every year as he starts school I write an "Introduction to Jon" letter to all of his teachers. His first year of High School, I do the same, and I find myself having to look back and pull out the important information from the last nine or ten years of his school life so his seven new teachers can have a jumpstart on knowing him.

I write first about his history, when he received his diagnosis in kindergarten and move on to behaviors. Most new teachers are very interested in what they should expect from my son in the classroom.

Up front I mention that Jon has come a long way. When he was little and used to get frustrated in class, he would lie face down on the floor and shut everything out, stiff as a board. When he grew older, he would lay his head down on the desk and cover himself with his arms, trying to block things out. As he outgrew that phase, he would bang the desk, or wall (a few times a person standing nearby) with his fist. He was quick to learn that this banging was not appropriate, especially banging of other people, and he replaced this with banging himself in the forehead. This is the most recent behavior we are still working on changing, and now he is pulling his hair on both sides of his head in frustration. A lot more appropriate than forehead banging, but still we are hoping to teach him to do something else.

Being a picky eater has also changed for him. Jon lived on chicken nuggets (in any shape) for the first six years of his young life. He has always eaten plenty of fruit, thank goodness, so nuggets, fruits and a multivitamin were his mainstay for a long time. Later he graduated to baked chicken, dark meat only, then turkey hot dogs. Of course he has always liked fast-food hamburgers and french-fries, but I wouldn't let him live on those.

Now that he is in his teens, he finally likes pizza, without having to drag all of the toppings off with a fork, and has gotten over his previous deathly fear of any little piece of cheese. He has a steak when we go out to dinner (which does get expensive), but we are so glad to see him get away from his chicken diet, so we fork out the money. He still eats any type of fruit we are able to get, and currently we are working on lettuce salads, plain, nothing on them. I recently listed for him the foods he used to not like, adding that this is why I still force him to try new things, or even old things, because his tastes do change. When he tastes something and says, "Hey! Not bad!" we are overjoyed!

Connected to food changes are changes in table manners. Eating out used to be such a struggle for us, not only because of his picky eating, but because of environment. When he was young we couldn't eat in a loud, busy restaurant because he had problems with the noise level, over-stimulation, and the facts that there were too many people and too much going on. There were times when something would upset him and he would end up lying in the booth or trying to hide under the table. Those were also the times when we got strange looks from other people, when they saw Jon bent over in his chair and halfway under the table. I never allowed him to get out of his seat onto the floor. As he grew older and the environment became too much for him, he would turn his back on us and look out of a window, or just away. I also didn't allow him to turn around in his chair, especially if there were other people close behind him, so often he would sit with his body facing forward and his head turned to the side, away from us. Facing us across the table for the entire meal was just too much for him.

We are still working on restaurant behavior, but at least he doesn't want to crawl under the table any more or lie down in the booth. When he starts to feel overwhelmed and begins to turn away from us in his chair, I tell him to face the front, and my husband and I don't talk or look at him for a few minutes so he can pretend he's not there. At first I thought this was only Jon-typical behavior, but I recently read in *Autism and Learning*, edited by Stuart Powell and Rita Jordan (1997), that quite a few autistic students with whom they worked have trouble facing a teacher one-on-one across a table, because the social contact is too intense for them. Ah ha! I realize that this explains Jon's restaurant behavior!

Another behavior I've recently noticed as changed, is Jon's sensitive hearing. At the beginning of kindergarten, before we ever had a diagnosis, Jon would not go into the gymnasium for PE. We took him to an ear doctor and were told that he had 10 percent greater hearing in both ears. We thought that this explained why he wouldn't go into the gym. So, I began working with him the first week of school. Twice a week when he had PE I was there, trying to edge him closer to being in the gym. In a month he was inside and with his fellow classmates partici-pating in the gym class. Later on during the year, when he had to attend school assemblies in the same huge gym we purchased "ear muffs" which helped muffle the sound enough that he could usually sit through the assemblies.

When we moved to a different school district, we had a lot more information and Jon was able to attend most events in the gym, and either used the ear muffs or not, depending on the noise level. When he entered Junior High he quit wearing them altogether and chose cotton balls instead, wishing to be less noticeable among the other students.

In High School, on the second day of school, they were having a Spirit Assembly where the entire purpose of the assembly is for the students to make noise and show their school spirit. Jon once again chose to use cotton balls, but *not* to sit with the Freshmen class. I don't know where he ended up sitting, but he said it wasn't that bad and he stayed for the entire assembly.

Is he completely over this noise issue? No, and I believe there may always be something in the environment that bothers him. He still tracks me down quickly if we are in a store and there is a shrieking child or crying baby, to say, "Let's split!"

Socially, he has changed for the better, but is still way behind his peers. He still wants to be a loner, and at one point I asked an expert at a conference if it was possible for my son to be not only autistic but a natural introvert too? Yes, was the definitive answer, and she pointed out that being an introvert was also typical of autism. Not only is he autistic, he enjoys being alone better than anything else. He loves it when company comes over to our house, but after greeting them or eating with them, he wants to go back to his space, alone. My husband constantly asks him, "Don't you want to hang out with other kids? Don't you want to have somebody over or go over to a cousin or friend's house?" His reply? "No, I want to be alone." And he is much too young to remember Greta Garbo saying those exact same words!

So for a parent who firmly believes that change is good, how do I make sure my son's behaviors continue to change so that he doesn't stagnate or stall out?

I admit as described in Cathi Hanauer's book *The Bitch in the House*, in our house I am that person. Someone needs to remind Jon constantly that banging yourself on the forehead because you are upset is not appropriate behavior. Someone needs to keep after him to try new foods, even if he swears up and down that one bite of macaroni and cheese will gag him and make him barf. Someone needs to teach him table manners, whether in public or at home, so that other people won't give him, or us, strange looks. And someone needs to encourage him to sit with the crowds, learn to deal with noise level, and get out of his bedroom, because life is on the other side of the door.

Do I get tired of being the bad guy?—Yes of course. Probably like most moms of typical children do too. Do I ever worry that my son will grow up hating me for all of my constant pushing and advice?—Yes. This thought has also crossed my mind more than once. The only thing I can do to keep that from happening is to be the bad guy in a loving way. Push him in a positive way, instead of negative. Be *the bitch in the house* without really bitching or nagging. Which is a very interesting tightrope to walk.

The Greek philosopher Heraclitus states that nothing is permanent but change. I would add that the one sure thing about my son and his autism is its changeableness, and perhaps a second, its presence. For although his autistic behaviors change, autism is always there.

Is there a way to chart Jon's behaviors in order to help others, or is this too individual?

chicken nugget #19

Three steps forward, one step back—not the latest dance craze

Why is it that my child seems to be going along just fine and then, bam! something happens…

I'm not the only parent who has wondered why it is that our children seem to take three steps forward and one step back. When Jon was in elementary school I noticed this almost immediately. We would be moving along, in a routine, things would be calm at school and something would happen. Jon would have what we call an "autistic moment" resulting in a meltdown or shutdown, and from that moment on a rough few days, sometimes an entire week would follow. We usually knew what caused the autistic moment, it was generally a reaction to something, but we couldn't figure out why they came with such regularity, three weeks (steps) forward one week (step) back pattern.

After attending another autism conference, I began thinking that perhaps this was food related. My husband is somewhat lactose-intolerant, perhaps milk products affected my son too. After all, there is a school of thought among parents who feel that certain diets can practically eliminate the autism. My husband and I, after looking into this, didn't feel this way, but I did take my son off milk for a trial run.

Things went fine. After about four weeks I put him back on milk on a Wednesday. Amazingly, we got a note home the same day that read: "Jon seemed easily agitated today and easily frustrated." The note at the end of the week stated: "This was a very difficult week for Jon. Are there some changes at home?" Ah ha! I thought. It's the milk.

The following week we had a short team meeting and I told them about my milk experiment. His aide said, "Well, if this is the case, please don't let him drink milk again, because last week was really a bad week for him." So, at about second grade, Jon stopped drinking milk and took a calcium-rich vitamin instead.

Did this solve the three-step pattern of development in his life? —No. He still went through this like clockwork, but I wasn't about to put him back on milk after seeing how for some reason it affected his system and his school day.

I wondered also if perhaps it had something to do with biorhythm? The *Oxford English Dictionary* defines this as "a recurring cycle in the physiology or functioning of an organism, such as the daily cycle of sleeping and waking." And there is also a system of thought that says we should try to find our natural biorhythm and try to schedule our life according to its cycle in order to be successful at anything we undertake. How many times have you heard someone say "my biorhythms are down today"? Maybe this was my son's natural cycle?

As he grew older, around Junior High, we tried milk again. He really seemed to miss drinking it once in a while or having it on his cereal. I set some limits and he got back on milk. This time we didn't get a note from school stating he'd had a really bad week, and the milk didn't seem to have any effect one way or another. Now I was stumped. It wasn't the milk.

In eighth grade, after having a rough week, his caseworker sent a note home suggesting that perhaps there was something going on at home? Was there some extra tension in the household between my husband and myself? "This does affect our kids," she added at the end of her letter.

After reading this to my husband, I burst out laughing. (Actually I had to laugh, or go choke the lady!) Was she actually suggesting that my husband and I were having marital problems? I looked at him, "Have we been tense or stressed or having problems this week?"

He thought for a moment. "No, not me? You?"

I shook my head, and we decided that we needed to see her that next Monday.

We showed up about 20 minutes before school and I let my husband do the talking (he was the good cop again). He explained to her, as we had done many times before, that for some reason, this was the way Jon is, three weeks up, followed by one down. We still had no explanation for it, but evidently this was pretty typical of autism and development. Before I could jump in, he told her we appreciated her concern, but we weren't under any stress the previous week at home and that this had just been one of "those weeks" for Jon.

"Okay," I said a few minutes later as we walked to the car. "You handled that the right way. But next time, I get to choke her!"

However, something my husband had said during the meeting began niggling in the back of my mind. Autism is a developmental disorder. My son's brain developed differently, and his developmental benchmarks were also different, whether completely missing or occurring at different times, or in the case of his speech, developing as echolalia. We knew all of this. These were the facts of his autism.

But what I was realizing was that my son was still developing wasn't he? This explained why he was always about two years behind his peers in social skills. His development in this area carried a two-year lag time. This also explained why the same year he had his first crush on a girl and wanted a girlfriend (seventh grade), he developed an intense interest in everything Muppets. His development was not level, straight, or typical.

Ah ha! I thought. Now I knew that this three steps forward, one step back pattern is because he has a developmental disability. It affects not only the way his brain developed, or his benchmarks as a small child, but every aspect of his life. He is developing in his own cycle, which because of the autism is a disabled cycle. Other parents of autistic children have talked about this three to one cycle too, so perhaps this is our children's cycle?

Or maybe not—because as fellow mom and author Gina Barnwell said on the phone one day, "When you've seen *one* child with autism, you've seen *one* child with autism." They are all, uniquely individual, even in their autism.

But as this school year begins, I know how to explain Jon's cycle a little better. I now realize that this different way of development is not the milk, not biorhythms or due to (bless that teacher!) marital tension in the home. This is Jon's disability (autism) revealing itself in all its true colors, three steps forward, one step back. It does sort of have a rhythm to it after all.

Can we learn to work with and predict this pattern for more success by planning tests during the good part of the cycle?

Chapter Twenty
Family members and autism
The Good, the Bad, and the Ugly

What can be done about unsupportive family members who do not understand?

This is the saga of the Good, the Bad, and the Ugly. Not a take-off on a spaghetti western, with guns and blood and guts, but a commentary on family members and how they relate to your autistic or Asperger's child. Will you find guns and blood? Only if the family situation erupts into a fistfight. Guts? Yes, it takes guts even to talk about one's family, but I look at this as just one more reality that needs to be discussed.

It's a given that not everyone in the world will be understanding about your child's disability. However, over the years, I've learned that even family members will have a few problems. I'm not talking about the initial shock or grief that families normally go through after learning of your child's diagnosis. What I'm talking about is the understanding of the dailyness of the situation. How do they treat your child? Do they try to work with your child's differences as you (or their teacher) would? Do they attempt to have the most patience possible in dealing with your child? Bottom line—do they respect your child's differences and treat him or her as a true family member? If your answer was no to any of these questions, then you too may be dealing with the Good, the Bad, and the Ugly!

The Good

One of the Good would have to have been my dad. When he was still alive, Jon was little and being tested and diagnosed. Dad admitted to not being able to see most of the problems with Jon that the educators saw, but he supported me 100 percent and read everything I passed his way on the topic. Of course, being close to 73 he was from the old school of learning, and for him there was nothing wrong with a child that a little extra love or extra discipline wouldn't fix, depending on what the problem was. But when it came to Jon, who was then seven years old, he read the books I gave him, and constantly reassured me that "Jon was going to be just fine!" A week before he died, he was the one who picked me up at the airport after I had attended yet another conference on autism. We talked about several things I had learned (it was at this conference I learned that Jon was pretty typical in his autism and food issues), and when Dad dropped me at my car he told me again, "Jon will be okay. He's got you. Just keep doing what you are doing." Many years now after his death, I can't help but continue to take his advice, for Dad was one of the *Good* ones!

My niece is also very Good. She is two and a half years older than Jon and was in High School while Jon was still in Junior High. She has been around Jon for only the past seven years, but she and her family lived with us for almost a year and she has attended the same schools as Jon throughout. She might not know all about autism, but she knows all about Jon. She knows that he is mostly an "A" student, she shares those same honors, and she also knows he has an aide to help him negotiate the regular classroom. She has never asked me questions about Jon, but she always shows extra patience with him, more so than any other teenager would.

Because of this, when Jon had his first boy–girl teenage birthday party, he invited her to be one of the girls (not telling her that the other girl he'd invited couldn't come), and she readily accepted. She showed up and didn't seem to mind the fact that she was the oldest of the other three 14-year-olds. She sat and watched Jon's video pick of the night *Ghostbusters* and didn't bat an eye.

After all of the chicken and french-fries were eaten and I was walking her to her car, she made one comment that proved she wasn't entirely clueless. Jon had invited a girl he has a crush on who also carries with her an IEP (although I didn't know this at the time). My niece made the comment, "I think they are perfect for each other. Don't they talk just alike?"

Yes. I had noticed these similarities between them also. She may not understand autism, but she does understand Jon, and she continues to, not only be understanding, but watches out for him now that they are both at the High School.

The Bad

These are the relatives who because of Jon's disabilities fail to treat him with—what can I say here?—extra kindness, or maybe they just fail to treat him the way I wish they would. These are the cousins who took everyone to the theme park except Jon one Sunday afternoon (Jon's favorite local theme park), which he's been to millions of times, rides most of the scary roller coasters, and generally has a blast and no "autistic moments." But because of his disability they took all of the other kids and family members except him. Did Jon know about this?—No. Because when I found out about it (they were all coming over later that night for dinner), I became so upset that I canceled the dinner. I wasn't about to cook a meal all afternoon for a group of people who couldn't take it upon themselves to ask Jon to go to the park with them. The whole situation made me feel very bad for Jon and I was glad he was unaware that they had gone without him.

Should I have been more understanding in this situation? I think not. A month before this, when this same family had gone to the same theme park, I mentioned that Jon would have loved to go and next time they went, to call him. I was told at that time, they didn't even think about it and would take him along the next trip. So when this happened again, I decided that they were just Bad in my book. Yes, they know about Jon's disability, but they don't respect my son enough to include him in family outings.

The Ugly

Fortunately, most of the family problems we have had fall into just the Bad category, but one year we ran into the Ugly. Sometimes you have it all together, all of your ducks are in a row, then you go someplace for Thanksgiving and realize who the real "turkey" is. This was our experience when we traveled out of town for Thanksgiving one year. We saw two sets of family members during this trip and when viewed side by side, the difference in the way they treated my son was a universe apart.

The first family we visited have very little understanding of autism, but they love Jon, and it is amazing what love does for a situation when understanding is needed. My brother-in-law and his wife extended great patience in listening to Jon give them facts about his current subject of interest, ad infinitum (zoos, I think it was), and they stood back and weren't overly protective as Jon enjoyed playing with his two young cousins aged two and seven. We had three wonderful days with them in San Francisco and were sorry to see them head back to Los Angeles, leaving us to visit a second family in San Francisco.

On the other hand, the second family we stayed with is where the situation got ugly. My husband's sister and her husband also had very little understanding of autism, but in addition what her husband lacked, was love for Jon. These are family members whom we rarely see and we were expected to stay with them Thanksgiving week. At the beginning of the visit we explained Jon's situation, and autism, and for about 48 hours things went peacefully. But it seemed that as soon as the turkey was gone, all patience went with it.

We were touring a winery in the Sonoma Valley when things changed. Jon, of course, was pretty bored with touring a winery, what neurotypical 14-year-old wouldn't be, much less an autistic youth. At one point we were standing and looking down on the storage barrels, and Jon pulled on my brother-in-law's sleeve to get him to move on. In that split second the pure look of anger and hatred on my brother-in-law's face totally shocked me. I quickly distracted Jon and told him he could tour the building with me.

When next we entered a small elevator to go from one level to the next, and Jon started to push the button, my brother-law folded his arms across his chest and said sarcastically, "That's fine. You want to be in control do you? Go right ahead!" Meaning, push the button. Jon was oblivious to his hateful tone, and I tried to laugh it off by saying something about "typical teenage behavior." Needless to say, the entire rest of the day, I placed myself as a buffer between Jon and this relative. Not only was what little patience he'd had with Jon long gone, but he began to be very hateful in everything he said to Jon.

Later, when we arrived back at their home, I did what any loving parent would do in my case. I told my husband we were packing and leaving immediately. When he looked at me in surprise, I explained what had happened, which he hadn't seen, and told him how I had tried to keep the two separated the entire day. He, also like any loving parent, agreed with me, and the next morning at 9:00 a.m. we were out of there!

The next day when I called my sister back home to tell her where we were, I cried when recounting how Jon had been treated. She immediately wanted to know if I had punched the guy out? (Remember my first reference to guns and blood?)

Alas, no. I didn't get violent. After all, this was a relative. But like I told my sister, lack of patience I can understand, goodness knows, we lose our patience with Jon. But being sarcastic, hateful, and mean-spirited is just plain Ugly in my book, and I will try to keep Jon from experiencing this as long as I live.

What is my motive for including this discussion about family? Is it to get my revenge for wrongs incurred?—I hope not. Because of Jon's autism, he is about 75 percent clueless to the way others treat him. (Bullying, unfortunately, he picks up on.) No, this isn't about revenge. I include this chapter because this is *reality*. How many times have we heard that you can't choose your family? You are born with them, and not every family member will be understanding when it comes to your child with special needs.

Thus, what is a parent to do?—My suggestion is keep in mind these three categories, the Good, the Bad, and the Ugly. Your family members, being only human, will fall into one of them, maybe even at different times in your child's life.

Celebrate the Good, cope with the Bad, and keep your distance from the Ugly!

Another word of advice from a book titled *Oh, Lord, I Sound Just Like Mama* by Lynne Alpern and Esther Blumenfeld; "With relatives, long distance is even better than being there."

Do I feel better, getting this off my chest? Was this better than resorting to blood and guts?

chicken nugget #20

Finding hope at the library

Recently Jon and I visited one of our favorite libraries. It has the best videos and DVDs available for check out. As Jon browsed the stacks, I stood at one of the tables looking through a pile of magazines, and overheard the following conversation between a boy of about ten and his mom.

"No, that's not autism, you are thinking of something else," she said.

My ears instantly perked up.

"But doesn't the face look different?" the boy asked

"No, that's Down syndrome," she replied. "Autism is when something happens to the way the brain is, neurologically, and they are sensitive to noise and sounds. Sometimes they get so frustrated, they may go off or bang their head."

By this time, I was grinning from ear to ear. I looked around the table at the kids who were with the two moms. None of them seemed disabled to me, so I thought maybe the boy was asking about someone he knew from school. Another child ran up to the table and the conversation shifted.

I sat down with a thud in the chair near by. This was wonderful, I thought. This mother was trying to explain to her son what autism was and did so pretty accurately. Someone had given her the right information to read, or she had done her own homework.

I was more than pleased. I was relieved. For once, in this situation, I didn't feel the need to butt in to their conversation and explain to them about my son and autism. They had the important facts down, and I couldn't keep the smile from my face. (If they noticed me at all, they probably thought I was a little bonkers!)

Later, I told my husband about what had happened. His reply was, "That's great." Yes, he's a man of few words. And as I was talking to him I realized that this was better than great—this was what I hoped for.

- I hope that the majority of the people in the world will finally learn what autism really is.

- I hope that the majority of parents can have the facts, as this woman did, to be able to explain autism to their children if ever the question arises.

- I hope that parents of children who are dealing with a diagnosis of autism (or Asperger's) can find the knowledge they need to understand, as best they can, their child's diagnosis.

- And I hope the children, youths, and adults carrying this diagnosis can grow to become happy, productive adults, in spite of their diagnosis.

Is this too much to hope for? Maybe, but if we don't have hope, we may give up. But on this day, I'm glad I didn't, because to my surprise I found some hope at the library!

Chapter Twenty One
Autism and religion

Can my autistic child have a real understanding of God or religion?

Once again I find myself tackling a difficult and personal topic. But if I don't try to answer these tough questions how can I expect others to even contemplate them?

First I must explain why this chapter is titled "Autism and religion" and not "Autism and God." In my mind there is a difference and always has been. I personally believe that you can have a strong, loving relationship with God, without religion. My definition for religion here would be organized religion, churches, synagogues, or mosques—religion, as in "I'm a _____" (fill in the blank yourself), as opposed to "I believe in God." After all, Albert Einstein once said that to him, "[his] religion consists of a humble admiration of the illimitable superior spirit who reveals himself in the slight details we are able to perceive with our frail and feeble mind".

I was raised in a church home, my husband was not. But by the time he and I had gotten together, I had seen too much damage done in the name of religion, and so had he. So when Jon was growing up, we too, as many families do, only visited a house of worship during the holidays, or for other occasions. Immediately, even before Jon's diagnosis, I knew he had trouble sitting through a church service, not to mention the impossibility of staying with total strangers in a nursery or children's church school.

But off and on we would try it, unfortunately usually coming away with a screaming or crying child. The music, the crowds, the lighting, numerous things would set him off.

After diagnosis we realized why this was not a successful environment for Jon, and I decided that teaching him about God, in my own mind, did not necessitate a visit to a house of worship. So, we stopped trying to fight that battle and concentrated instead on giving Jon a strong faith in a loving, forgiving, understanding God.

Of course this is easier said than done because how do you explain to a child who has difficulty with abstract ideas, that there is a God, who created the Universe, and that you can pray or talk to this God when you need help? It is still an ongoing process for him to grasp.

However, recently I realized he may be getting an inkling of things. We were on our way home from a shopping trip right before Christmas. We had walked through the crowded mall, not necessarily to buy, but to enjoy the Christmas decorations and the holiday atmosphere. When we walked by all of the little kids lining up to see Santa I couldn't help but say, "Hey, there's Santa! Do you want to go see him?" Jon had done this every year up until about fifth grade. "Very funny, Mom," was his reply.

Quite out of the blue, he said, "Mom, if there was a Santa, you know what I would ask him for Christmas?" Here we go, I thought. Another list of items.

"What?"

"I'd ask him for answers. You know. About the mysteries of life. About God and the gods and the Bermuda Triangle."

I was almost at a loss for words, but finally managed, "Yeah, that's a good idea. I think I would ask for answers too." My son was growing up. He was searching for concrete answers to abstract ideas and mysteries.

I wasn't surprised at his question "*about God and the gods.*" He had already told me that he'd had a conversation with his "only" best friend about God. This other boy is a great kid and his family are real churchgoers. They have invited Jon several times to attend with them and I've always left the decision to him. He has always said, "Naaa," after remembering the organ music and the singing. But he has attended several youth activities with his friend.

One day he came home from his house and said, "Kevin told me that all of the Greek and Roman gods are wrong."

"Oh, yeah?" I said, trying to think how to answer this one. "What did you say?"

"I told him that different people call God different names. And that the Greek and Roman gods were what they called Him."

I beamed at him. "What did he say?"

"He said they were pagan. What's pagan?"

Hmm, another tough one. "Pagan is what some people call other religions because they don't believe the other person's religion is right," came my first response, and as I was quickly thinking of how to rephrase this, he interrupted me.

"I think the Greek and Roman gods were real too. You know, just another name for God."

We then discussed this a little more at length, delving into the development of religions over the ages, and I hope he got most of what I was saying. But what amazed me most about this conversation, was that Jon was proving to be a "free thinker." This was his best friend, Kevin. He and Kevin had disagreed about an issue, and Jon had decided that he didn't want to think like Kevin. I suddenly felt reassured that as I had been trying to teach Jon things like, "life is not black and white, good or evil, completely right or completely wrong," he was developing a habit of trying to think for himself and sticking to his own way of thinking. For a son who learned to speak through echolalia, (imitating sentences he heard elsewhere) this was very important. I didn't want him growing up with a rote learning of God. I didn't want my son, who could be a great parrot, learning to parrot a belief in God. And it seemed, at this point, that he was actually doing some thinking about it.

As I prepared this chapter I re-read several articles and papers on the topic of autism and religion. The Autism Society of America posts two papers, one titled *The Christian Perspective*, by Terri Connolly (2005) and the other *The Jewish Perspective*, by Joshua Weinstein (2005). Both of these contain wonderful information to help parents wishing to involve their child in a religious community. I totally respect and commend parents out there who make this choice for an active religious life with their autistic child. Once again, it must be an individual choice.

I also read several posts by autistic individuals themselves. Some of them were very anti-religion, others had grown up in a house of worship and felt at home in the religious community of their choice. The key here, of course, is *choice*. Just because your child or youth or young adult is autistic, doesn't mean that you take away their choices. Jon is high-functioning autistic/Asperger's. He has matured and become more capable of making an informed choice, instead of simply echoing or parroting what he hears. I am very proud of him, and I will encourage him to develop this habit of "free thinking." His developing a belief in God is a very positive thing in his life.

Alas, on a sad note. A year ago there was a small article in the local paper that caught my attention. It was only an inch or so long, but the words have stayed with me since I read it. "Young autistic boy smothered to death during a prayer session," it began. The minister of a church had been trying to exorcise the autistic demons from the boy and had smothered the boy to death. The man was found guilty and sentenced to two and a half years in prison and seven and a half years state supervision. The boy's father was quoted as saying that this was only "minor justice."

I cried when I read that article, and I cry now. How many atrocities have been done in the name of religion over the years, *any religion*? And I thank God that I've tried to teach Jon about a loving, forgiving, understanding God, and have left religion out of it. As I have always said when it comes to working with our children, different things work for different individuals on the spectrum. And just as autism is a very individual disability, so is one's belief in God.

Will my child ever wish to be a part of a religious organization?

Angels by my side

What keeps me from running screaming into the night?

After asking Emily Perl Kingsley what kept her going, it seems I needed to answer it myself. She ended by saying it's important not to dwell on what her son *might have been*, but rather on *what he is*.

I agree 100 percent with this. When Jon was diagnosed ten years ago, my husband and I soon realized that we had to focus on the positive. If we constantly kept the thought in our minds "Jon has a disability," we would soon be buried under that thought. So we tried to keep the thought "Okay, he has a disability, but what can he do *in spite* of this disability?" We weren't denying the autism, but we were working with Jon, and for Jon, in spite of the autism. This too could bring you down and depress you, but you must do something to keep from, as Emily said, staying in bed and pulling the covers over your head, or, as I say, running screaming into the night.

What else gets me through?—The angels I seem to have by my side.

One of my closest angels is my sister, Jan. She has taught public school for over 20 years, and although she too had to relearn the definition of the scary word "autism," she is one of my best supporters. She reads what I send her to read, advises me on how to deal with teachers when I need it, gives me a shoulder to cry on when necessary, and is always available for therapeutic shopping trips. It's not often that a woman has a best girlfriend and a sister all rolled into one, much less an angel too. But I do!

We also had an angel in Jon's taekwondo teacher. This young man enjoyed working one on one with Jon, seeing Jon imitate the karate routine as they stood side by side. Later, when we had dropped out because of a misunderstanding with the owner, I ran into him on campus. "I'm so glad to see you again," he said. "After you and Jon stopped coming I quit, because I saw the way the owner had treated Jon, and I disagreed with her approach. I just wanted you to know that." Ah! I knew liked this teacher for some reason.

As I was working on my first book I ran into an angel at the local K-Mart about once or twice a month. She was a cashier and an artist: painting and drawing. Every time I saw her she asked me, "And what about your book?" I would explain where I was in the process, and she would patiently listen as she rang up my items. Then she would say, "Oh, you will get it published. I think you are doing something just great for other parents." This angel I've lost track of since her family has moved out of the area. But wherever you are, "Margaret-angel, you were right! Thank you for your interest and your kind concern."

I saw an angel by Jon's side the other day. She was at a Christmas party with one of the clubs that we have "forced" Jon to join in High School. I was sitting and observing, trying to stay out of the way. All of the students had brought gifts to exchange and they were sitting in a group on the floor, drawing numbers to go pick gifts. The idea of the game was that they could then take another student's gift if they wished. Jon wanted so much for his friend, a girl, to get his Christmas gift, but she had forgotten her gift at home and couldn't take part. Just before things started, I whispered in his ear, that he could pick his own gift and then give it to her. This seemed like a great idea to him, and this is what he did. A few of the other kids in the group immediately protested and jeered at him that he had picked his own gift, but an angel came over and said, "Leave him alone! He can pick his own if he wants to!" She sat down beside him on the floor and helped him unwrap it. Then she quieted the other kids as he carried his gift over to his friend and gave it to her. Later when I asked Jon what this girl's name was, he said he didn't know. Angel was good enough for me.

Jon and I met an angel the other night, dressed in jeans with spiked hair. He was cutting Jon's hair. It was a salon we had never been to, the only one that had evening appointments. He listened to Jon tell him about the trip to Hawaii we had just returned from. He listened to Jon give him the history of Walt Disney, dates and all. He cut, and he a-huh-ed and he listened. When he had finished, my son looked in the mirror and whispered, "Perfect! Can we come back here?" He then hurried out to the car while I paid. The first words out of this angel's mouth? "He is amazing! He's a walking computer!"

I laughed. "Yes, you may have noticed. He happens to be autistic."

The young man nodded his head. "I used to work at Lakeway [an outpatient hospital for teenagers dealing with mental disorders, depression, drugs], and believe me, I've seen it all. But your son! Wow! He's amazing!"

Thank you for reminding me! He is isn't he?

A nice surprise is that Jon's caseworker at the High School is also his angel. We noticed from the beginning, from our first "getting to know Jon" meeting that this woman had her act together. She is a take-charge, no-nonsense type of person, but, most importantly, she has studied her stuff and she understands about autism, and Jon. When we were dealing with Jon and rudeness, as in, calling the teachers names like "*jerk, dork, free-loader,*" I e-mailed her to tell her that we agreed with her 100 percent that this is not acceptable behavior. But I was reminded of what Dr. Temple Grandin had said about autistics saying things without thinking. I mentioned what Dr. Grandin had said about the brain developing differently so that any filtering or advanced thinking was messed up. She e-mailed me back immediately and said she too had thought about what Dr. Grandin had said about "blurting." How she used to blurt until she lost a job because of it. She said she wanted to give Jon alternatives to blurting his feelings, so that he would be able to function better in the world. And also, she thought that getting used to apologizing for this was also a good thing to learn. I e-mailed her back that it was so nice to be on the same page, and told her she was a gem in my son's life. An angel at school! Who would have thought.

Finally, I have to mention the constant angel by my side, Jon himself. Oftentimes he does something so unexpected that makes me laugh or makes me stop and think. When I go out of town and leave him with his dad, he grabs me and hugs me on my return as if I'm a lifeline. Not that he doesn't like staying with his dad!

When I grow quiet, thinking, or writing in my head, he asks, "Are you all right?" He is the one who hits three bookstores with me in one day, sitting and reading, in hog heaven like me. And when he says something funny and we both laugh so hard, I see my only son, a gangly teen with a great sense of humor. In that moment, the autism disappears and he is simply *the angel by my side.*

Chapter Twenty Two
Shadow dancing

It's an abnormal world I live in. I don't belong anywhere.
It's like I'm floating down the middle. I'm never quite sure
where I am.

(Arthur Ashe, tennis great)

Is there really a difference between being lonely and being alone?

We arrive home from our family vacation to Hawaii. It was a wonderful trip and I am excited about putting our digital pictures on my computer. I load all 142 of them and then sit down to watch a self-made slide show presentation. There we are, taking the island tour, going through the Dole Pineapple Fields, standing on rocky beaches and sandy beaches. One picture of Jon catches my attention and I pause my computer to get a closer look. Ah, yes. These are of Jon running on a sandy beach. My husband stood back and took them, so they are also of myself, watching Jon. I smile as I remember that right after this sequence of pictures Jon got hit with a huge wave and was wet up to his shorts. One shoe and one sock got drenched, and he was very stressed about it the rest of the tour.

But something else catches my eye and I scroll back to one picture in particular. This is one of Jon, playing with a wave. The wave approached, Jon moved back, closer, back, closer, back. This picture seems oddly familiar to me, as if I've seen it before? Do we have any other pictures of Jon playing with waves?

Then I see it. This picture does resemble another.

In a dusty photo album I have a picture of Jon when he was about three years old. Four years before the diagnosis of autism entered our life, and the only thing we knew was that Jon's speech was coming slower due to, as we were told, the fact that our family was bilingual. This picture is taken outside of our home in sunny California. Jon is on the driveway, alone, and he is having the time of his life. Before I took this picture I remember wondering what he was doing. Then as I watched, I realized he was actually playing with his shadow. He would look over his shoulder, watch his shadow move this way and that, laugh in delight, and move across the driveway. My son was *shadow dancing.*

Right after diagnosis I came across this picture again, when we were talking about developmental milestones. I realized then that Jon absolutely loved playing by himself. Even at the age when he should have been interested in playing with others, he was content to play alone. When we moved back to the mid-west from California and I entered him in a "mommies' morning out program," I would find him in the gym when I arrived to pick him up, and he would be having the time of his life, playing by himself. When he was having difficulty in kindergarten, when they were just beginning to test him, I would sit and watch him on the playground, alone. At that time he enjoyed the swings or walking the railroad ties around and around the perimeter of the playground.

Now, even in High School, Jon eats his lunch usually sitting alone. When he and his best friend get together at each other's homes, oftentimes they play alone, one on the computer, one on the video game player, in the same room, but alone.

My husband and I ask him about this constantly. Doesn't he want to go hang out with other kids?—No. Wouldn't he like to spend time with a friend?—Not really. Please come out of your room for a while and talk to us. He does so, very reluctantly and then getting him to talk of course is like pulling teeth. My husband finally asks him, "Do you like to be alone?"

"Well, yeah," he replies.

"Why?"

"Because people bother me," he says, and that is just about as far as we get. Which of course is like a *duh* moment for us. Of course we knew this. He's been this way his entire life. We were only hoping that he could perhaps explain it to us a little more.

I see this picture of my 15-year-old, playing with the wave and I wonder if he will be alone his entire life?

As usual, I go to the internet and begin my search. What I find is a link to an article by Stephen Shore, titled "Dating, Marriage and Autism", which appeared in ASA's publication *Advocate* (Shore 2002). Here

Stephen talks about being on the spectrum, dating, and for him, eventually marriage. What greatly interested me is how he explained about different types of dates and how he always expected the women he dated to be the socially aware ones and be able to tell him what they expected from him. At the end of this article he advises parents to encourage their children to get involved in activities that interest them so they can learn to be part of a social group which would hopefully lay a foundation towards a closer relationship.

After reading through this article, I searched a little more and found a web page titled *Welcome to Chris and Gisela Slater-Walker's Website* at www.Asperger-marriage.info. I read through this site about this married couple, who have also written the book *An Asperger Marriage*, and I find a sense of humor and some very practical suggestions for making things work. At the same time I also realize that any marriage is work, not just one where one of the partners is on the spectrum.

From this article I do what I call surfing and find several links to home pages, chat rooms, blogs, and discussion boards, for the sole purpose of helping adults or young people talk about, deal with, and understand relationships (from a spectrum point of view). I don't enter into any of these. Alas, I'm a neurotypical parent, but I found about 50 of them in about 30 minutes.

What does all of this surfing tell me? It tells me one very important thing—there is a chance that Jon will wish to move into a closer relationship when he gets older. There is a chance that he may begin dating, find a friend, and that this friend may become a significant other in his life. *When* this will happen, I couldn't predict. After all, autism is so individual. *How* is another unknown—the couples I noted had met their spouses or significant others in many different and various places. Whether he will make a success of this relationship is another question that I can't answer and whether he will live happily ever after is another.

After reading Stephen Shore's article, looking through Chris and Gisela's web page and surfing the net, I don't come away with a lot of solid answers, but I do come away encouraged. For I have learned that my son, who happens to be autistic, has a future. Just like any neurotypical out there, Jon will grow up, mature, and live out his life, either with a spouse or significant other, or alone.

Right now he is still shadow dancing, but he is not lonely. He still enjoys his aloneness. Why?—Well, *because other people bother him, Dad!*

But later on, as he grows up, hopefully goes to some type of college, and hopefully finds his niche in a job somewhere, maybe by then he will no longer wish to be so alone. Hopefully, he too will find happiness with someone else.

Until that time, I must be content to watch him enjoy his aloneness, enjoy his shadow dancing. And I must try to understand that, for him, there is a difference between being lonely and being alone. It seems that Jon is not experiencing the first one yet.

Is this too much to hope?

chicken nugget #22

Serendipity—the sauce
for those nuggets!

Growing up in a Protestant church I remember reading a small book about serendipity. I can picture the book in my mind, and I think it must have been when I was in elementary school, because it was an oversized book, with very few words and colorful pictures. If my memory is correct, this book set out to explain that God is in the little things. These little things are not necessarily miracles, according to the church I was raised in, but they might be called "serendipitous events." According to Rodale's *Synonym Finder*, *serendipity* is synonymous with fortuity, fortuitousness, happenstance, Lady Luck or Dame Fortune. Thus, I grew up believing that when things mysteriously come together for the good, it is serendipity.

Recently I read that in 1949, psychoanalyst Carl Jung coined the word *synchronicity*. "Telepathy, clairvoyance and precognition are all synchronicities—meaningful coincidences between person and events in which an emotional or symbolic connection cannot be explained by cause and effect", meaning more than just happenstance or Lady Luck. For Jung, this is how the universe is connected, which is similar to modern chaos theory, that if a butterfly flaps its wing in Tibet, that one ripple in the atmosphere ultimately affects the entire universe.

Jung's idea is a lot larger than my idea of serendipity, but I try to wrap my brain around synchronicity, and ponder it off and on, as it gives me something to explain the unexplainable.

There was the time I was working on my first book, *Parent to Parent*, and I wanted to use a poem titled *Welcome to Holland*. This poem was one of the first things I'd read after Jon's diagnosis which touched me, and gave voice to how it really felt when we were told that Jon was autistic.

I used the poem as I was drafting the book, not knowing at the time who the author was. I'd copied it down years before and the author's name wasn't on my copy.

At this same time I was a substitute for the school system, filling in for the High School Spanish teacher who had taken a group to Spain for two weeks. One morning I opened up my classroom and stopped at the table in front of the room to pick up the morning's attendance. Imagine my shock when beneath the attendance record I found staring up at me the complete *Welcome to Holland* poem with the author's name, Emily Kingsley. I felt a tingle as I picked the poem up and flipped it over. Unbeknownst to me, the Spanish teacher's child had Down Syndrome. Emily Kingsley's son also has Down Syndrome, and the newsletter was reprinting her poem on Holland.

I stood looking at the poem for several minutes. Now how did this poem get to me right when I needed to use it in the chapter I was working on? Right when I needed to know the exact phrasing and who the author was? After the tingling stopped I remember thinking, "How serendipitous, if unexplainable."

Later, when I told my engineer-trained husband what had happened, he said, "Well of course the office worker left the mail on the teacher's table and this was where the newsletter came from."

"Yes, but why did it come this week, while I was subbing for this teacher, while I was writing a chapter using the Holland poem? Why now?"

He could only shake his head in wonder, while I nodded mine in excitement. Synchronicity, I think? Is everything really connected?

These memories came to mind yesterday. We were doing some work at our real estate office, getting ready to convert the old motel rooms into individual office suites. When the city inspector showed up to inspect the new electric meters, the only room that had power was the room I use to write in. As I opened the door for him, he paused and said, "Oh, are we interrupting someone here?" I glanced inside and saw my books lying on the motel bed, papers and printer set up on the table.

"No, this is where I write," I told him and proceeded to explain to him that I wrote about my son's autism. My first book was out and I was working on the second.

"Ah," he said. "That's interesting. My wife and I fostered two young children, both of whom were diagnosed autistic."

We then stood for 15 minutes or so and had the "typical" autism conversation, he asking questions, me trying to answer them to the best of my knowledge. He finally remembered to inspect the electric, and on the way to his car said he would look for my book at the bookstore.

Over the years, many more events have occurred that are just as unexplainable. I'm 100 percent sure that I'm not the only person who has these experiences.

I told my husband about this one too, and said that when the inspector came back to re-inspect, he may have more questions for me.

"Isn't it a small world?" I said. "What are the chances?"

My husband, the engineer, didn't have an answer. Another serendipitous moment.

Do I believe as Jung did that there is synchronicity in the world? That all things are really connected to each other in some way?—Maybe. Do I believe the teaching of my church, that God is in the small things?—Perhaps.

However, this is what I know I believe. I believe we need to be awake to the moment. We need to be open to see connections, to interact actively with what is going on at this point in time. If I walked around in a cloud, not caring to connect with life, with others, I would have missed out on too many serendipitous moments.

Like the time I was in a small town on a craft-shopping weekend with my sister, and I felt compelled to give the lady at the bookstore my card and tell her about my book. She mentioned immediately that the Mayor's son, age 14, was Asperger's and she always wondered how to talk to him. We had a nice little chat then and there, and she said she would talk to her boss about possibly getting my book for their small shop. What a moment!

The nineteenth-century physicist John Tyndall wrote in his book *Fragments of Science*, "Life is a wave, which in no two consecutive moments of its existence is composed of the same particles." Serendipity or synchronicity, a small miracle, fate or Lady Luck, it doesn't matter what we call it. Living *in the moment* is what counts. I hope I continue to catch that wave!

Epilogue

An epilogue should be a postscript, coda, conclusion, last and final words, or...a *swan song*!

Does it ever get easier?

This question was recently put to me. The "it" in the question being our experiences of parenting a teenager with autism, "it" meaning, being an advocate for my son, dealing with the daily issues of autism in our life. I paused and really contemplated my answer before saying, "No, not easier. Just different."

As I write this epilogue, I get a call from one of Jon's High School teachers. She tells me that his civics grade has dropped considerably from an A– to a C–. She explains that she, along with all of his teachers, will be available for teacher/parent conferences this coming Friday, and perhaps we can all meet and do some brainstorming. She said it seemed that when Jon took the last test not only was he unable to finish it, but he also told them, "Nope, I don't know any more. I'm finished," when they encouraged him to think some more. She said this was so unlike Jon, who excelled in her class.

I thank her for the call and tell her we will be there. Then I write in my calendar the time, along with the note that the Spanish teacher had e-mailed the week before saying Jon was having more difficulty right now, and remembering that the English teacher had given him an F on his poetry test. (When I asked Jon about this test, he said maybe he didn't understand some of the questions, because he *thought* he knew the information.) I add the English teacher to my list and as always the science teacher who he has been struggling with since the first of the year.

No, it definitely doesn't get easier. Because now we are dealing with autism *and* teenage issues. Soon we will be dealing with autism and young adulthood, hopefully autism and college, autism and the workplace.

But, as I told the person who asked me the question, "Life is really okay. Jon has difficulties, and will continue to have difficulties, but he is a happy young man, most of the time."

And isn't this what parents of neurotypical children, teenagers, and adults aim for: happiness, most of the time? If so, then we have succeeded with Jon, and Jon too has found success.

My interests continue to lie in the same questions: What can I know? What ought I to do? What may I hope? This is the only way to live our lives with autism and the teenage years, and continue to count ourselves successful.

At the moment, I will put the questions to rest on this thought from an unknown source: "...peace does not mean to be in a place where there is no noise, trouble, or hard work. Peace means to be in the midst of all of those things and still be cool, calm and collected in your heart. That is the real meaning of peace." As always, I wish you knowledge and *this* kind of peace, no matter where you are.

References

Alpern, L., and Blumenfeld, E. (1986) *Oh Lord I Sound Just Like Mama*. Atlanta: Peachtree Publishers.

Attwood, T. (1998) *Asperger's Syndrome: A Guide for Parents and Professionals*. London: Jessica Kingsley Publishers.

(autism-society.org) (2005) Connolly, T. *The Christian Perspective*. Weinstein, J. *The Jewish Perspective*. Website posts.

Buscaglia, L. (1982) *Living, Loving and Learning*. Thorofare, New Jersey: Slack, Inc.

Buscaglia, L. (1983) *The Disabled and Their Parents*. Thorofare, New Jersey: Slack, Inc.

Caws, M.A. (2002) *Vita Sackville-West: Selected Writings*. New York: Palgrave Macmillan.

Grandin, T. (1996) *Thinking in Pictures*. New York: Vintage.

Grandin, T. (1999) *Choosing the Right Job for People with Autism or Asperger's Syndrome*. www.autism.org/temple/jobs.html

Grandin, T. (2004) *Teaching Tips for Children and Adults with Autism; Recommendations For Students with High Functioning Autism*. www.teacch.com

Heather (2004) www.geocities.com/EnchantedForest/Glade/6190/sped_jargon.html

Hogan, K. (n.d.) *Recommendations for Students with High Functioning Autism*. www.teacch.com/highfunction.html

Ingold, D. (1999) *How Do I Tell My Child About His [Her] Diagnosis?* www.asw4autism.org/ASSEW/ASSEWnews199.htm

Jackson, L. (2002) *Freaks, Geeks and Asperger Syndrome*. London: Jessica Kingsley Publishers.

Jordan, R. and Powell, S. (1997) *Autism and Learning*. London: David Fulton Publishers.

Klein, L. (2002) *Asperger's Students in High School*. http://www.lbpsb.qc.ca/~asdn/ LesKleinTalk.html

Powell, S. and Jordan, R. (eds) (1997) *Autism and Learning: A Guide to Good Practice*. London: David Fulton Publishers.

Pritikin, L. (1999) *A Policy of Inclusion: Alternative Foreign Language Curriculum for High-Risk and Learning Disabled Students*. ERIC Data Base, ED 428586 FL 025785. Reproduction supplied by EDRS 2002.

Ramani, Dr.N. (2004) *Empathy finding offers autism hope*. BBC Online News, UK Edition. news.bbc.co.uk/1/hi/sci/tech/3690763.stm

Saint-Exupéry, A. de (1967) *Wind, Sand, and Stars*. Pennsylvania: Harvest Books.

Sayers, D.L. (1935) *Gaudy Night*. London: Hodder.

Shore, S. (2002) 'Dating Marriage and Autism.' *Advocate 4*, 24–27.

Siegel, B. (1996) *The World of the Autistic Child*. New York: Oxford University Press.

Smith Myles, B. (2000) *Asperger Syndrome and Difficult Moments: Practical Solutions for Tantrums, Rage and Meltdown*. London: Jessica Kingsley Publishers. (First published in the USA as *Asperger Syndrome and Rage*.)

Thoreau, H.D. (1971) *On Walden Pond*. New Jersey: Princetown University Press.

Tyndall, John (1897) *Fragments of Science*. New York: D. Appleton & Co.

Wagner, S. (2004) *Middle School Madness and High School Hysterics*. Emory University. Power Point Presentation.

Weinstein, M. (2006) *The Imaginative Prose of Oliver Wendell Holmes*. Missouri: Missouri Press.

Wheeler, M. (2004) *Getting Started: Introducing Your Child to His or Her Diagnosis of Autism or Asperger Syndrome*. www.iidc.indiana.edu/irca/generalinfo/ getstarted.html

Woolf, V. (1916) *Hours in a Library*. London: Times Literary Suplement.

Woolf, V. (1925) *Mrs. Dalloway*. London: Harcourt.

Subject index

Author index